ULTIMATE

Fishing Adventures

100 Extraordinary Fishing Experiences From Around the World

Henry Gilbey

This edition first published 2012
© 2012 Henry Gilbey

REGISTERED OFFICE

John Wiley & Sons Ltd, The Atrium, Southern Gate, Chichester, West Sussex, PO19 8SQ, United Kingdom

EDITORIAL OFFICE

John Wiley & Sons Ltd, The Atrium, Southern Gate, Chichester, West Sussex, PO19 8SQ, United Kingdom

For details of our global editorial offices, for customer services and for information about how to apply for permission to reuse the copyright material in this book please see our website at www.wiley.com

Library of Congress Cataloging-in-Publication Data is available
A catalogue record for this book is available from the British Library.

ISBN 9781119962663 (pbk.); ISBN 9781119968009 (ebk.)
ISBN 9781119968016 (ebk.); ISBN 9781119968023 (ebk.)

Graphic Design by Holly Ramsay
Set in 9.5/13.5 TFForeverTwo
Printed in Italy by Printer Trento.

Cover image: © Henry Gilbey

Wiley Nautical – sharing your passion.
At Wiley Nautical we're passionate about anything that happens in, on or around the water. Wiley Nautical used to be called Fernhurst Books and was founded by a national and European sailing champion. Our authors are the leading names in their fields with Olympic gold medals around their necks and thousands of sea miles in their wake. Wiley Nautical is still run by people with a love of sailing, motorboating, surfing, diving, kitesurfing, canal boating and all things aquatic.

Visit us online at www.wileynautical.com for offers, videos, podcasts and more.

Ultimate Fishing Adventures

100 Extraordinary Fishing Experiences Around the World

Henry Gilbey

Dedication

To my wife and two girls – travelling the world and doing what I do
is just amazing, but the best bit about it is coming home and being
enveloped by my family when the front door opens. You are the best
and I am the luckiest man alive – Henry Gilbey

Greenland

Iceland

Best times to fish
The short summer season, with August being the prime time

Fishing methods
Fly and lure

Getting there
Generally from Iceland

Tips and tricks
It is vital to take serious mosquito prevention methods – sprays, nets, anything that might keep them away from you

ARCTIC CHAR, GREENLAND
A short summer season beset with perfectly crazy numbers of fish

Time it right and the sheer numbers of Arctic char you can catch in Greenland can literally take your breath away. Generally, anglers interested in fishing for these char will fly in from Reykjavik in Iceland, so it is more than possible and also well worth combining a salmon fishing trip in Iceland with an Arctic char extravaganza in Greenland.

It is actually possible to fish for Arctic char from the coastline in early summer. From June to July, when the char have moved out of the rivers and lakes and into the fjords, you can fly fish or spin for these fish close to the river mouths. But from July into August, these vast waves of Arctic char migrate up the rivers on the high tides, so for the most part you will be fishing the areas around either the river mouth or more typically where the river meets a lake. The best all round time for chasing these prolific fish is in August when the greatest concentrations of fish have moved up the rivers and, importantly, when there are fewer mosquitoes around. On the whole,

a Greenland Arctic char is going to weigh from 1–5lbs, but they can reach nearly 10lbs from time to time. Although the best of the fishing is in the middle of summer, local temperatures average around 10°C; hardly on the balmy side, but wrap up warm and this might well prove to be one of those world class fishing trips that is for some reason not well known about.

A river such as the Kangia is very cold and very clear, and in season there will literally be thousands and thousands of char in here. Fish of over 10lbs have been caught, and you will be able to see the fish you are going for. To fish many of the best char locations in Greenland will often require a combination of vehicles and then walking in, with fishing camps mainly being very remote. When the fish are on, they will happily take both wet and dry flies such as the Silver Doctor and Polar Shrimp. Char are known for very aggressively taking an unweighted fly that you skip across the surface, so you need to make sure that you up the breaking strain of your leader to cope with such savage takes. It is not considered desperately hard to catch over 100 char in a day's fishing.

Summer might well be short, but the reason that Greenland is such a prime destination for Arctic char is the sheer number of healthy rivers full of so many fish. A local nickname for an Arctic char with those red bellies and dark backs is 'Father Christmas'.

Best times to fish
The salmon season is
1 June to 30 September

Fishing methods
Fly fishing

Getting there
Various ways. By air
from Montreal to
Gaspé and Bathurst.
Alternatively, how about
the night train from
Montreal to Bonaventure
for a bit of fun

Tips and tricks
Do exactly as your guide
says with regards to flies
and where to cast them

GASPÉ PENINSULA, CANADA
One of the best kept secrets in Atlantic salmon fishing

The Miramichi river system might well be the most famous Atlantic salmon fishery on the east coast of Canada, but the stunning and wild Gaspé peninsula is utterly unique when it comes to its own salmon fishing. This peninsula extends around 220 miles into the Gulf of St Lawrence, and what makes the salmon fishing so different and attractive is the fact that the main rivers fished here are incredibly clear, to the point where you are actually sight-fishing to salmon most of the time. Don't make the mistake though of thinking that just because you can see the fish they suddenly become much easier to catch, because this is not the case at all. However, to see individual fish and indeed shoals of them hanging in water sometimes so clear that it looks like there is none there is just incredible. To actually know that the fish are there certainly helps boost the confidence levels when chasing Atlantic salmon, yet for some reason this wonderful part of Canada does not seem to receive the same kind of salmon-related publicity that other parts do.

The fishing on these rivers in Quebec is run by the local ZEC, a not-for-profit organisation set up by the government to carefully monitor and manage local fishing and hunting activities. Fishing

permits are not expensive and are allocated by ballot. Rivers such as the Grande Cascapedia, Bonaventure, St Jean, Petite Cascapedia, Dartmouth and York are all split up into zones or beats and the ZEC manages access so that there is never any kind of over-fishing pressure on these waterways. There are a number of fishing lodges with fully guided outfits that can take salmon anglers out on the main rivers, but also fly anglers are perfectly entitled to enter the ballot system themselves. With this much water, though, it does make sense to work with local outfitters who know exactly where the salmon are in the rivers from day to day. Some of the local guides have been working on these rivers nearly all their lives.

Three of the main rivers (Bonaventure, Grand and Petite Cascapedia) start from the Chic-Choc mountains and run cold and clear all year round. The Grand Cascapedia can produce salmon to over 40lbs. It is really quite something to watch when perhaps 30lbs of perfect Atlantic salmon refuses your flies for so many casts, but then suddenly charges across a pool and engulfs one. Sight-fishing to salmon is about as exciting as it gets, but the trick then is to calm your racing heart and go at it with a methodical approach that you might adopt when fishing on a Scottish or Russian salmon river, for example.

Canada
Miramichi river
USA

Best times to fish
Early summer into autumn is the best time for the larger fish, but spring usually throws up the numbers

Fishing methods
Fly fishing

Getting there
Easy access from airports such as Moncton, Halifax and Fredericton

Tips and tricks
Go prepared for some potentially seriously cold weather in the spring

MIRAMICHI RIVER, CANADA
The east coast of Canada could not be more wonderfully different to the west

There are few more famous areas to go and fish for Atlantic salmon than the Miramichi river system in New Brunswick on the east coast of Canada. It was in the mid-19th century that sport fishing for salmon really began to take off, and even in the 1960s it was estimated that the salmon run was around one million fish. The runs now are not as prolific as they once were, but still the Miramichi system is the place that produces the largest numbers of Atlantic salmon anywhere on earth. There are some stringent conservation efforts going on which are slowly but surely improving the runs of fish year on year. The rivers of New Brunswick average around 30,000 plus salmon per year to fly anglers.

Numerous salmon fishing lodges along the Miramichi provide fully guided fly fishing. Many of the guides come from families who have been guiding salmon fishing for generations. It is in fact law that anglers who come from outside of New Brunswick must be accompanied by a

guide. The Miramichi has taken a lot of the traditions from salmon fishing in Scotland, in that many stretches of the river system are privately owned and then leased by various fishing clubs, outfitters and guides.

Salmon fishing starts on 15 April, with a run of fish that have mostly entered the river system late the previous summer and then remained under the ice. This is the time of year that a fly angler can expect to catch the largest numbers of fish. Much of this early season fly fishing is done from a boat. It is in mid-June that the summer influx of fresh fish really kicks in, and this run usually lasts until about the end of September. This is the best time to be in with a chance of landing a 30lb plus Atlantic salmon on the fly, and much of the fishing is either from the bank or via wading. Bag limits and/or catch and release regulations change each year, depending on the numbers of salmon that are counted entering the rivers. There is also a run of sea-run brook trout that tend to enter the system in late May and on into June.

Subject to which part of the system you end up fishing, you may need to be able to use both single-handed and double-handed fly rods to properly cover the water. Wade fishing will often require the use of a double-handed rod, but when fishing for the spring fish earlier in the season from the boat, then a single-handed rod is more applicable.

Canada
● Kasba Lake

USA

Best times to fish
Around mid-June through
to the end of August

Fishing methods
Lure, fly and bait

Getting there
Anglers tend to fly into
the Kasba lake area out
of Winnipeg

Tips and tricks
Take a look at the fly-out
options to even more
remote waters if you
want to, although there is
no real need with all that
water around

KASBA LAKE, NORTHWEST TERRITORIES, CANADA
Big, wild, and full of serious numbers of hungry fish

The huge Kasba lake is just one of any number of lakes and rivers contained within
the wild and vast Northwest Territories. An area of around 500,000 square miles, but with a
population of roughly 50,000 people, it goes without saying that accessing most of the fishing
requires a serious logistical undertaking. Luckily, though, there are several professional operators
who can assist any angler with an urge to fish in the absolute wilderness.

Kasba lake is huge by most standards, but despite measuring 55 by 25 miles, with over 2,000
miles of shoreline and a healthy ecosystem full of a significant amount of smaller fish and crustaceans, it is only the 28th largest lake in Canada. There are also masses of islands, reefs, rivers
and streams for some wonderfully varied freshwater fishing. Lake Kasba is a very good place to
target big northern pike, lake trout and some serious Arctic grayling. The grayling around here are
generally accepted as being the largest Arctic grayling in the world. The fish are very well looked
after, with Kasba Lake Lodge having implemented a strict catch and release policy since 1975.

Perhaps the most exciting time to fish for the huge numbers of northern pike are when the ice melts in spring through to early August, when you can target the fish in the shallows on all manner of lures. Pike have been caught in Kasba lake to over 35lbs. Later on in the season these fish move into deeper water with plenty of cover, and this is when anglers tend to either troll or use large lures.

Lake trout need large waterways to grow really big, and on Kasba there are very good numbers of these incredible fish in the 20 to 50lb class. The biggest fish are usually taken via precise trolling methods or otherwise with large spoons and deep diving lures. You can often catch sizeable numbers of smaller lake trout in the shallow water bays where at times they will come and take off the top, but otherwise the more regular casting and jigging methods work well.

The Kazan river, which flows out of Kasba lake, is home to some of the best Arctic grayling fishing there is. A combination of serious numbers of fish and a healthy proportion of them coming in at over 3lbs is the reason why this is about as good as it gets on both flies and light spinning outfits. There are 4lb plus grayling taken every year.

Fly anglers should note that northern pike and lake trout can be very successfully targeted in the main lake. When the cisco baitfish are spawning in the shallows, for example, through August, you can catch plenty of lake trout which are of course well switched on to these ready meals.

Best times to fish
A short season, generally mid-September until the end of October

Fishing methods
Fly fishing

Getting there
A roughly four-hour drive from Terrace or Smithers, but the lodge can arrange for a helicopter transfer

Tips and tricks
Take some time to really get to grips with double-handed or Spey casting

BELL IRVING AND NASS RIVERS, BRITISH COLUMBIA, CANADA

A serious place to go and lose yourself to the drug that is steelhead fishing

Some 220 miles north of Terrace on the quiet Stewart-Cassiar highway, there is a remote heli-skiing lodge that for a few weeks each autumn offers fly fishing for the majestic steelhead on the stunning Bell Irving and Nass rivers. This is some of the most pristine and out of the way steelhead fishing there is, and with a high average size of fish and such perfect fly fishing conditions, it is no wonder that anglers return year after year.

The Bell Irving is a tributary of the extensive Nass river, and it's in the autumn that the river flows tend to be the most stable and consistent for steelhead fishing. The guides at the lodge generally use shallow-draught jet boats to access and navigate the numerous fishing spots, and many clients also opt for perhaps a couple of days' helicopter access to the upper stretches of the nearby Nass. It is perfectly possible to take a 15lb plus steelhead from the Bell Irving, with the most numbers of fish appearing from about mid-September and into October. True 20lb plus chrome steelhead are always on the cards. Average size fish from the Bell Irving might run to 8-10lbs, and from the even more remote Nass this might jump to 12-14lbs. You can get all kinds of weather at this time of year in British Columbia, so it is important to prepare for the worst and then layer down if and when it warms up.

The Bell Irving is just about the most perfect river for fly fishing in that there are numerous fairly shallow pools and runs that can be easily wade-fished. Although the areas of the river you fish are not particularly wide, it does help to be able to effectively cast with a double-handed rod to help avoid the trees behind you that often come right down to the riverbank. Takes from these very unpressurised steelhead are often on the savage side and, as much as it is important to be able to put a long line out across the cold waters, more than 50% of the steelhead caught here are taken on the dangle. Patience is the key when fly fishing for these magnificent ocean-going rainbow trout, but then just spending time amongst such a place is arguably as special as hooking one of these fish.

The Nass river is more unpredictable than the Bell Irving when it comes to flows and clarity, but with so much water surrounding the stunning Bell II lodge, there is usually somewhere to fish. This is true wilderness fly fishing, and at any time you might encounter moose, black and grizzly bears, wolves and eagles. Paying close attention to your guide goes without saying.

Canada
Skeena watershed
USA

Best times to fish
Steelhead and salmon all run at different, very specific times of the year

Fishing methods
Fly, lures and bait

Getting there
Terrace is a good base. Easy connections from Vancouver

Tips and tricks
Over 50 per cent of steelhead come 'on the dangle'. Be in no hurry to get your fly out of the water to cast again

THE SKEENA WATERSHED, CANADA
Iconic steelhead and salmon fishing in the wild heart of British Columbia

Arguably the river system that is the world's most famous destination for steelhead and Pacific salmon fishing, the Skeena river and its tributaries, such as the Kalum, Nass and Kitimat, offer some truly outstanding fishing nearly all year round, if you can brave the cold of early spring and late autumn (fall) into winter. The Skeena itself, at 354 miles long, is the second longest river in British Columbia, and over five million fish return to spawn in these cold waters each year. It is well known when the principal runs of the different fish occur, and there is a professional network of fishing lodges and guides who can take anglers out fishing with fly or conventional gear. Much of the fishing is based out of the town of Terrace, and to fish these rivers in the wilds of British Columbia is surely one of the great fishing experiences on this earth.

The Skeena watershed is generally accepted as offering the best fly fishing for steelhead in the world. These powerful ocean-going rainbow trout run back up the rivers at various times of year to spawn, with the autumn run being the most notable for visiting fly anglers. A spring run of steelhead takes place from around March to the end of May, and then the autumn (fall) run kicks in from around mid-August through to the end of the year. The most prized steelhead are those that are fresh from the sea and have a strong silver sheen to their body. These fish are hugely powerful and many fly anglers can't help but fall hopelessly in love with fishing for them amongst such beautiful surroundings. The whole 'steelhead–bum' culture centres around the wilderness that is British Columbia.

The five species of Pacific salmon all run the Skeena watershed at different and generally very precise times of the year. The largest king or chinook salmon run the river from around mid-April through to the end of August. These fish grow seriously big and are almost horribly powerful. A chinook that weighs over the 30lb mark is known as a 'tyee', and every year there are chinooks over 60lbs taken from the Skeena river system. These mighty salmon can grow to over 100lbs and are often called spring salmon too because they return to the rivers for spawning before any of the other Pacific species.

The other Pacific salmon species fished for are the powerful coho, which are known for their aggressive nature (mid-August to mid-November), chum or dog salmon (mid-June to end of September, in the Kitimat especially), pink or humpback salmon (June to end of October, the smallest of the Pacific salmon species), and then sockeye or red salmon (mid-June to end of September). Time your fishing right and you can catch steelhead and various salmon species on the same trip. Don't ignore the spring run of steelhead that can just about coincide with the first chinooks running the system.

Canada
Copper river

USA

Best times to fish
The beginning of August to mid-October, but the best times for dry fly fishing will fluctuate within this period

Fishing methods
Fly fishing

Getting there
You can fly from Vancouver to Terrace very easily

Tips and tricks
Make sure you really source the best local guides to put you on to fishing like this, and then work closely with them to get your dry fly in front of an angry steelhead

COPPER RIVER, CANADA
Catch it right, and this might just be one of the ultimate steelhead fishing experiences

A part of the mighty Skeena watershed, the Copper river can, at very specific times of the year, offer the steelhead angler something wonderfully different; that is the opportunity to catch these magnificent ocean-going rainbow trout off the top on skated dry flies. The intimate Copper river runs into the Skeena just a few miles outside of the town of Terrace, which lies about 600 miles north of Vancouver.

The opportunity to fish dry flies for steelhead depends very much on the conditions, and the 'season', as such, runs from around the start of August to the middle of October. The water temperatures are usually about the right level to keep the steelhead in an aggressive mood and willing, at times, to take flies off the top, but if they are not going to come up for the dries then you can always fish for them more conventionally with weighted wet flies.

There are two principal sections to the Copper river that are fished by anglers, but it is more than worth searching out good local guides who have proper access and can offer clients time on

the river. The lower to mid sections of the river are for the most part accessible by truck along the logging trail that runs for miles and miles into the wilds of British Columbia. Many of the walks or near-climbs down to the river, which shimmers far below in the deep valley, are better suited to the fitter or more adventurous anglers, but the chance to fish these kinds of waters are well worth the extra effort. The upper sections of the Copper are accessed via helicopter, which obviously pushes the prices up. The beauty of the whole Skeena system is that in a land where river levels can fluctuate from day to day with rain and snow, there is always going to be somewhere that a good fly fishing guide can take you for a bit of world class fishing.

Dry fly fishing for steelhead is all about the presentation. Due to the generally lower water levels and the fact that the Copper is in most places a smaller river, you can usually fish with lighter rods when using dry flies. The cast is aimed just downstream from across the river, and then as that line begins to tighten, you help the fly literally wake along the surface. However, it is important not to get that fly really racing over the water while your belly of line starts to straighten out in the flow. If a steelhead does come up and smash your fly then you would be doing well not to fall off your rock from the shock.

Best times to fish
June to the end of
September

Fishing methods
Fly and lure

Getting there
Most anglers would
fly to Kobuk from
Fairbanks, or via
Kotzebue from
Anchorage

Tips and tricks
Watch out for bears.
Alaska offers some true
wilderness fishing

KOBUK RIVER AND
SELAWIK DRAINAGES, ALASKA, USA

**The Kobuk river and Selawik drainages offer the best
sheefishing in the world, but most people have never
heard of this magnificent freshwater fish**

Often referred to as the 'freshwater tarpon' or 'tarpon of the north', the sheefish, or inconnu, is a species of fish that can be caught in some of the more remote northern Alaskan waterways. Once hooked, these fish will sometimes literally cartwheel clear of the water, almost like a tarpon does in saltwater. The sheefish is the largest of the whitefish and can reach over 50lbs. There are smaller populations of sheefish in the Yukon, Kuskokwim and Koyukuk river drainages, but the largest numbers of them are to be found to the south of the Brooks range of mountains. The Kobuk river and the Selawik drainages produce the biggest fish, and there is every chance of taking 30lb or even 40lb plus fish from these waterways. If you get it right with the fishing, then

you can sometimes catch huge numbers of gloriously distinctive and handsome sheefish, but it does all depend on fishing with the right people in the right places and at the right time.

Sheefish will generally hug the bottom of the rivers as they move up, and they tend to feed in the slower and deeper water. Fly fishermen will usually have to fish with weighted flies and sinking lines to get down to these fish.

The sheefish start to migrate to their spawning or feeding grounds soon after the ice begins to break up after the long Alaskan winter. Some fish will go to spawn whereas others will move to feeding grounds, and the distances they travel vary greatly depending on the river systems they are moving through. The sheefish that swim into the Koyukuk river, for example, will end up travelling over 1,000 miles for their spawning. Sheefish prefer to spawn when the water is fairly cold in September and October, and then they quickly move back down the rivers to return to their wintering grounds in Selawik lake.

The Kobuk river is in north-west Alaska, just inside the Arctic Circle. Few anglers seem to know that these magnificent sheefish even exist, but the Kobuk river valley also fishes well for northern pike, Arctic grayling and chum salmon in season. The grayling fishing can be particularly out-standing. Some hardy anglers will even jig for sheefish through the winter ice out on Selawik lake.

Canada

● Fraser river

USA

Best times to fish
Mid-April to the
end of November

Fishing methods
Bait

Getting there
Easily accessible
out of Vancouver

Tips and tricks
For such a docile looking
fish, sturgeon in fact will
often run very, very fast
when hooked. They will
also jump, so you will
need to hang on!

FRASER RIVER, CANADA

Within easy distance of Vancouver lies some of the most dramatic river fishing there is. Sturgeon pull serious string

The mighty Fraser river is the longest river within the British Columbia region, running to nearly 1,000 miles in length. This famous river holds the five Pacific salmon species at fairly specific times of the year, but also within its waters roam one of the true giants of the freshwater world, and each year more and more anglers are heading to the Fraser to do battle with a fish that could end up weighing over 1,000lbs. The white sturgeon has somehow come through past periods of severe overfishing to remain well established, and there are numerous guides who are willing to take clients out to try and catch one of these monster fish. For a long time now the Fraser river sturgeon fishery has been a 100% catch and release operation, and it does seem that numbers of fish are on the up. As is the case throughout much of the world, the more anglers who fish for a particular species, the more valuable it becomes and therefore the more protection is often afforded to it.

Sturgeon are a wonderfully unique species. The sheer fact that you could fish a river and end up hooked into a quarry that might measure more than 10ft long could be somewhat alarming. But it is also certainly humbling to realise that a sturgeon can be more than 150 years old and will have spent those years feeding mainly via scent or touch due to having very poor eyesight. Most sturgeon will weigh between 50-250lbs, but every year some real giants will get caught.

The majority of the sturgeon fishing on the Fraser river takes place from Hope down to the river mouth, and these fish can be caught in a wide variety of depths and locations. It is advisable to fish with a good local guide who will cut out so much potentially wasted time. The Fraser river is huge, and to the uninitiated it will, of course, look rather daunting, but sturgeon tend to favour the slower running water. These are potentially monstrous fish, and therefore the actual fishing gear is often on the somewhat substantial size to deal with the sheer pressure. However, for large fish, their actual bite can sometimes be very gentle.

Successful baits depend on the time of year you are fishing, but they will include lamprey eels, sockeye roe and various parts of the salmon, and then perhaps chum salmon roe as the season heads on into autumn or fall. Sturgeon tend to be very inactive in the depths of winter, but this being Canada, that's the time to break out the steelhead fishing gear and chase the magnificent ocean-run rainbow trout instead.

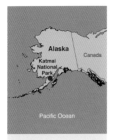

Alaska

Katmai National Park

Canada

Pacific Ocean

Best times to fish
June to September, but it depends on which salmon species you might want to focus on. Different rivers peak at different times as well, so liaise closely with your chosen outfitter

Fishing methods
Fly, lure and bait, subject to who you fish with

Getting there
Generally fly from Anchorage on to King Salmon airport, and then your outfitter will take over from there

Tips and tricks
Immerse yourself completely in the whole rafting, camping and sharing experience to really get the most of the trip

KATMAI NATIONAL PARK, ALASKA, USA

If you only go fishing in Alaska once, then think seriously about doing a float trip in Katmai National Park

Many people say that if you were to do one single trip to Alaska in your fishing life then it should be a float trip down one of the majestic rivers of the vast Katmai National Park. Comprising over 7,000 square miles, the park offers fishing for the five Pacific salmon species together with other fish such as the Dolly Varden and big rainbow trout. It is one of the world's finest places to truly immerse yourself in a proper wilderness experience, where the actual fishing could perhaps merely be an excuse for going there. And if you want to see plenty of bears, then this is the place. Within the park are the famous Brooks Falls, where every year large numbers of grizzly bears congregate to feast on the salmon that are running the gauntlet to head up river and spawn.

A float trip down one of the rivers such as the Alagnak, Kulik, Nonvianuk, American Creek, Grizzly Creek, Moraine or the Karluk might best be described as an overall attack on the senses.

There are no longer many places on earth that are devoid of human pressure, but parts of Alaska are so wild and remote that any angler could well be forgiven for forgetting about fishing at times to instead just soak up the ambience.

In general a float trip starts with a flight that goes deep into the Katmai wilderness. Many trips originate out of King Salmon airport, with the name itself providing a clue as to how important these fish are to Alaska. To see a part of the world where the fish run in such incredible numbers is something that no angler could ever forget. Float trips revolve around camping along the river you are going to float down, and although this may not compare to the comfort of a lodge, there is something wonderfully satisfying about rafting and camping your way down. Waking up to the great outdoors and then having breakfast along the riverbank before going fishing is something that only camping can give you, and there are several very experienced outfitters who run these kinds of trips throughout the season.

When the various salmon species are really running, the fishing is not exactly that tough or technically demanding, but many anglers choose to concentrate on the Dolly Varden, grayling and big rainbow trout in particular. There are also some lake trout in a number of the lakes. If you really want to get away from the crowds for your fishing then this might be one of the ultimate ways of doing so.

Christmas Island

Indian Ocean

Best times to fish
A genuine all year round fishery

Fishing methods
Fly fishing

Getting there
Flights to Christmas Island depart from Honolulu in Hawaii

Tips and tricks
Don't forget about the triggerfish on the flats as they can be hugely challenging and fun to fish

CHRISTMAS ISLAND, PACIFIC OCEAN
With all those magical flats spread out before you, it's like Christmas every single day

There cannot be many saltwater fly anglers who have not heard of Christmas Island and its plethora of flats fishing. World renowned as one of the most prolific bonefish fisheries on earth, the vast myriad of flats, channels, cuts and offshore waters also produce various trevally species (giant or GT, bluefin and golden), triggerfish, plenty of different reef-dwelling species (grouper, snapper etc), as well as a chance at wahoo and tuna. But it is as a sight fishing destination for bonefish and trevally for which Christmas Island is most well-known, and with over 250 square miles of shallow bonefish flats surrounding the remote island, there is rather a large number of fly fishing options on offer.

Christmas Island is a long way from anywhere. Situated in the South Pacific, it lies 1,200 miles south of Hawaii. The fact that what is the largest coral atoll in the world sits only 200 miles from the Equator makes it a truly year-round fly fishing destination, and with numerous endless flats that seem almost custom-designed for sight fishing, you can understand why so many fly anglers return again and again to this Pacific paradise. As on the remote Seychelles atolls, the bonefishing

is done on foot, and perhaps this is part of the appeal. You slowly and deliberately wade the shallow sand and coral flats with your guide, on the lookout for signs of bonefish. You will see an abundance of fish in the 2–5lb range, and you will often get the chance to put a fly in front of a magical 10lb plus bone. Whether you can control your nerves and excitement levels, however, is another matter entirely, but then this is what big bonefish in skinny water can reduce almost any fly angler to. The rare but highly sought-after golden trevally can sometimes be seen tailing on the flats, and they too can be caught on bonefish tackle. If you hook one, they are going to run harder and faster than even a bonefish does, so be prepared. Make sure you have plenty of backing on your fly reel and hang on tightly.

Christmas Island is one destination where it is more than possible to tangle with a savage giant trevally (GT) on the flats, and while nowhere on earth perhaps can rival those outer atolls of the Seychelles for sheer numbers and size of fish, the Christmas Island waters also hold an impressive amount of GTs of all sizes. In general, the GTs will seem to appear as if from nowhere in the many lagoons or the deeper edges of the shallow bonefish flats, so it always pays to be ready for the different and potentially much larger fish that might turn up. The aggression with which these monsters can hit a fly is unlike anything that a first time saltwater fly angler will have ever seen.

Montana
DePuy spring creek
North Dakota
Idaho
Wyoming
South Dakota
Nevada
Nebraska
Utah
Colorado
Kansas
Arizona
New Mexico
Oklahoma
Texas

Best times to fish
There can be good fishing
all year round

Fishing methods
Fly only

Getting there
Near to Livingston
and Bozeman

Tips and tricks
Scale right down and
fish very stealthily

DEPUY SPRING CREEK, MONTANA
Perhaps the best spring creek fly fishing in the whole of the US

Situated in the stunning Paradise Valley, south of Livingston in Montana, the small DePuy natural spring creek supports a very healthy population of wild rainbow, brown and cutthroat trout. Its backdrop comprises the imposing Absaroka mountains. Paradise Valley has three principal spring creeks, these being the DePuy, Nelson and Armstrong. There is a wonderful symmetry between DePuy and the mighty and world-famous Yellowstone river, which runs directly behind this small wild creek. A great place to fly fish virtually all year round, the DePuy spring creek is technically the bottom half of the Armstrong creek. Even in the depths of winter you can fish the DePuy due to the waters running at a fairly constant temperature. Unlike the Yellowstone that is of course affected in early season by snow-melt from the mountains, the DePuy spring creek is not. There is actually a strong argument for the DePuy spring creek being one of Montana's best true winter fisheries, and with the extremes of weather that this stunning state has, this is really saying something. Only about 45 minutes away from all this fly fishing is one of the entrances to the famous Yellowstone National Park, and anybody who makes the journey to this part of the world would be seriously remiss not to spend at least one day in the park. You never know, you might even see Yogi Bear if you keep your eyes peeled! Since, however, Yogi Bear is not actually real, then at least watching a bison cross the road in front of you is something that you will never forget.

As much as the trout on the DePuy are generally pretty used to seeing anglers, make no mistake that some serious technical fly fishing is needed if you want to really succeed. The upper part of the creek tends to offer the most challenging fishing. Here you can truly stalk and target individual trout, whereas further down is generally where the fish are a little less spooky. The creek ranges from around 10 to 25m wide, depending on which part you are fishing, and a diverse habitat includes numerous deep runs, riffles and even a spring fed pond that can be fished effectively from the boat.

If you can deal with the weather variations, you should seriously consider fishing the DePuy in the spring time when some big rainbow trout from the nearby Yellowstone River enter the DePuy to spawn. April is notably a month of change in this part of Montana, but expect proper snow showers and storms at this time of year and beyond. The DePuy is a private fishery and you need to buy a permit. Rod numbers are strictly controlled.

Summer tends to be when most anglers will fish the creek, but there can be some really good fly fishing into October when the brown trout start to spawn and the reed beds are still in good condition. Weather changes fast in Montana, and a day on the DePuy can really present some true fishing challenges from beginning to end.

Washington
Montana
North Dakota
Bighorn river
Idaho
South Dakota
Wyoming
Nebraska
Nevada
Utah
Colorado
Kansas
Arizona
New Mexico
Oklahoma
Texas

Best times to fish
Good fly fishing all year round, depending on weather conditions. August is accepted as being the most consistent month

Fishing methods
Fly fishing

Getting there
Fort Smith is a good place to stay and use as an access point for the fishing. It is about 90 miles from Billings in Montana

Tips and tricks
If you are going to fish there in winter, go prepared for some potentially very cold weather

BIGHORN RIVER, MONTANA
Thirteen miles of blue ribbon, American trout fishing heaven

The Bighorn river is generally accepted as being one of the finest and most consistent trout rivers in the whole of the USA, with many miles of blue ribbon water, as it is known, and a very significant amount of insect life. The majority of the trout fishing takes place in the 13 miles below the Yellowtail Afterbay Dam in Montana, for this dam tends to regulate flows and thus produce some perfect trout habitat and fishing conditions. With all the extreme weather patterns that can be found in this part of the world, it seems pretty exceptional that the Bighorn provides truly year-round fly fishing for trout. After this almost perfect stretch of water, the Bighorn begins to slow down, with irrigation pulling a lot of water from the river, but good brown trout fishing is still available further downstream. During the summer months the lower half of the Bighorn tends to be more of a catfish and bass fishery, although there are still some large trout around in the autumn (fall) and spring, in particular. Also, there are far fewer anglers here than on the more famous upper reaches.

The Bighorn river contains more large, 15 to 20 inch trout than any other river in the US, and with an almost crazy population density estimated at 3,000 to 5,000 trout per mile, you are more often than not going to have a very good day's fly fishing. The downside though is that a stretch of river like this receives the most amazing amount of fishing pressure; indeed during summer you can expect to see literally dozens of specialist drift boats making their way down that famous 13-mile stretch, as well as any number of fly anglers fishing from both banks. But outside of summer (July–September), the volume of fishing drops off, although you can expect to see anglers out on the river even during winter in favourable fishing conditions.

A strong blue-winged olive hatch takes place mostly around midday from April until early June, and both dry flies and nymphs can work well. Early July is about the little yellow stonefly hatch, but as good as the fishing might be with the right weather, August does tend to give the best fly fishing of the year. During this month, the pale morning dun hatch is coming to an end, but it overlaps with the caddis hatch that will run into September, and without doubt the evenings are when the hatch is at its strongest. There might be an incredible population of trout on this stretch of the Bighorn, but with the numbers of anglers fishing it you must remember that these brown and rainbow trout see a lot of flies through the course of a year. The better the presentation of your fly, the greater the rewards.

HENRY'S FORK, SNAKE RIVER, USA

If there is a trout fishing heaven on earth, then this might well be it

Easily one of the most well-known trout rivers or streams in the entire USA, Henry's Fork is a tributary of the perhaps equally famous Snake River. Sometimes known as the North Fork of the Snake River, or even just The Fork, it is in north-east Idaho and runs for around 150 miles out of Henry's Lake. Henry's Fork offers some of the finest dry fly fishing water ever, and the abundance of big wild rainbow trout and prolific insect hatches draw anglers here from all over the world. Below the dam at Henry's Lake are 15 miles of what is known in the US as 'blue ribbon' trout water, and it is a catch and release only fishery.

Box Canyon lies below this first 15-mile section. It is a 3-mile long stretch of Henry's Fork, but within these turbulent few miles is where you will find some of the best fishing for the big rainbows. Most fly anglers will use a boat to fish this part, for here there is faster water with plenty of rapids and features to hold the fish. June and July tend to be the optimum times to fish in Box Canyon; be sure to take a selection of streamers and nymphs for use in the more agitated water.

'The Ranch' (Harriman Ranch) is a famous stretch of Henry's Fork. It is a slow and wide part of the river, with a bed that is densely covered with weed growth. There are plenty of smaller rainbow trout, which are not usually that hard to catch, but the big, 20 inch plus rainbows are really going to take a degree of fly fishing skill to entice them to take a dry fly. The River Test in the UK, for example, generally has a strict upstream dry fly policy, but on Henry's Fork it often pays to ignore this more traditional sentiment and sometimes allow your fly to go out across or even slightly down and then swing. Pale Morning Duns, Mahogany Duns and Blue Winged Olives can work well on occasion. Autumn or fall is a good time to fish here, especially because most of the crowds have disappeared after the holiday season. There are numerous spots you can safely wade-fish from, and with all those weed beds, it is often the case that you will be essentially fishing blind to fish that are tucked away in the beds. The Ranch section might well get a fair amount of fishing pressure in season, but this tends to be where those largest trout are going to come from. There are plenty of guides and fishing lodges available, and you can keep well up to date with the fishing reports online.

Best times to fish
July to November

Fishing methods
Lures, bait and fly.
Serious gear required

Getting there
Easily accessible from
all over the upper east
coast of America

Tips and tricks
Work very closely
with your skipper,
especially when a big
fish is hooked up

CAPE COD, USA
You don't know the meaning of fishing pain until you have hooked into a huge bluefin tuna

Cape Cod is, of course, very well known for the quality of the striped bass fishing to be found in its surrounding waters, but at certain times of the year the bluefin tuna, one of the largest and most powerful fish to swim the seas, comes close in to this shore. It is a formidable fishing quarry, and the prospect of tangling with a 500lb plus bluefin can leave anglers who know all about it sometimes shaking with a mixture of fear and excitement.

Of course, there is a huge worldwide problem with the bluefin tuna stocks, but for some reason the rich waters off Cape Cod have seen what seems to be a fairly healthy influx of bluefin tuna of all sizes. Strictly enforced rules and regulations have been implemented to govern what anglers may and may not land. The famous Stellwagen Bank is where most of the biggest tuna are caught, but it is situated nearly 15 miles off the coast, and with some changeable weather this is more usually fished by the larger sport fishing boats. However, you will find plenty of other tuna fishing in the inshore waters around Cape Cod.

When tuna fishing, you cannot expect the same movements of fish as in the previous years. The relatively inshore waters to the east of Plymouth, though, have been fairly consistent in providing good tuna fishing during the autumn or fall. More specific locations include Buzzards Bay and the Race at Provincetown.

It is generally accepted that the absolute largest bluefin tuna are taken on livebaits, which are fished under balloons or even kites. Bait species include mackerel, porgies and menhaden, and their availability depends on season and weather. Gear is usually 80lb or even 130lb class boat rods and fighting chairs. This is more akin to preparing for battle than going fishing, but a large bluefin tuna's power is insane. The 'smaller' bluefin tuna can often be fished for via speed or vertical jigging methods, as well as on heavy fly fishing tackle if the angler is seriously experienced at tangling with such fish. One of the most exciting ways possible to catch a bluefin tuna is to take it off the surface on a popper, much like you would with a GT in the Indian Ocean. If you or your skipper can find bluefin tuna busting bait on the surface, then this is the time to cast poppers at them. Imagine sometimes many hundreds of pounds of single fish smashing into your lure and you might understand why these fish can literally beat up anglers so badly. Pure adrenaline and no small amount of pain are involved. These fish can swim at over 40mph.

Best times to fish
Some good fishing all
year round, especially for
snook, redfish, snappers,
sea trout and groupers

Fishing methods
Fly, lure and bait

Getting there
Just off the coast, west
of Fort Myers, Florida.
There is a toll-bridge
over to the islands

Tips and tricks
Do not even attempt to
go fishing without first
buying the correct fishing
licence. Local tackle shops
will be able to help you

SANIBEL AND CAPTIVA ISLANDS, USA

The warm, shallow waters of the Gulf of Mexico are teeming with hard-scrapping fish

Situated in the Gulf of Mexico, just off the coast of south-west Florida, the 12 by 3 mile Sanibel Island and its smaller 4 by ½ mile sister, Captiva Island, offer all kinds of saltwater fishing. With a myriad of inlets and mangroves, these waters are famous for some outstanding snook fishing practically all year round. Together with an abundance of snook, there are plenty of species such as redfish, tarpon, seatrout, jacks, barracuda, cobia and sharks.

The extensive Gulf of Mexico is pretty unique when it comes to sport fishing, for you can easily be 30 miles or so offshore and still the water will be no deeper than perhaps 50ft. There are no reef systems as such in these warm waters, but there are numerous wrecks, structures and artificial reefs, as well as plenty of smaller bait species on which the larger predators feed. Sanibel and Captiva Islands provide excellent access to the Gulf, but so much of the fishing that these islands are known for takes place close inshore.

Snook are a hugely sought-after species, and there are numerous fishing guides who can take you out looking for them. Sight fishing to fish like these in shallow water is hugely exciting. However, within these warm local waters is also one of the largest and healthiest populations of redfish in Florida. You can often see redfish tailing like bonefish or permit, in that they are feeding head down in water so shallow that their tails come out of the water and almost act as a 'flag' to a light tackle angler. Snook, though, are masters at lurking quietly in the mangroves, and they are often a very easily spooked fish. A stealthy, measured approach usually pays dividends.

These two islands are on the migratory path of the huge waves of tarpon that swim up this coastline, and from about mid-April and on into July you can cruise the shallow waters looking for these immense sporting fish. As well as boat fishing around here, there is also plenty of outstanding fishing to be had from the beaches. The best of the sport is usually around first and last light when the place is at its quietest, and you can wander around areas such as Bowman's Beach and the West Gulf Drive with lures, flies or live baits. Many anglers will cast-net for their own live baits, but fishing in the US is a very organised business, and you can always pick up what you need in the local fishing tackle shops. There is not one month of the year when the fishing around Sanibel and Captiva Islands is not worth seriously considering.

Best times to fish
For the best striper fishing off the shore, fish from late September into November

Fishing methods
Mainly lure and bait, but fly fishing works well from some of the locations

Getting there
Montauk is on the end of Long Island, not far from New York

Tips and tricks
Get properly geared up against the elements and you will fish significantly better

MONTAUK, LONG ISLAND, USA
One of the main places to be to latch onto the autumn or fall run of striped bass

Say the word Montauk to anybody with any interest in surf fishing or striped bass and it's likely that legendary locations such as the Lighthouse and Turtle Cove will come to mind. This is one of those places that is almost like some kind of shore fishing Mecca, but you should know that when the stripers are in and feeding it can get really crowded. As with a lot of fishing though, it's often the more popular and well known locations that are fished the most, but if you go looking and speak to the right people then you can usually find somewhere less crowded and hectic to fish. Crowds of anglers, however, often mean crowds of fish around here. Known almost universally as striper fever, these magnificent bass instil a passion bordering on obsession amongst hardcore surf anglers, who will often brave treacherous, cold conditions to cast lures and baits for these fish.

Montauk is situated right on the end of Long Island and sits directly in the path of the annual striped bass migration. Warmer Gulf Stream currents and strong tides help to move shoals of bait around this historic peninsula, and from late September through November, huge shoals of striped bass will come close inshore to gorge on them. Montauk is one of those places where a 'blitz' will often occur within casting range of the shore. With fishing, a 'blitz' is when predatory fish feed very hard on smaller baitfish and in their frenzy to do so, the predators literally drive the fish to the surface and then almost boil in amongst them as they gorge on the bait. At times the striper blitzes that happen off Montauk can almost defy belief, and you can bet that when they happen an army of 4x4 vehicles and anglers will be chasing them down. The term 'combat fishing' is sometimes used to describe fishing almost shoulder to shoulder into a blitz. The best of the striped bass fishing off Montauk waters is a brief season, during which the surf junkies are drawn here like bees to honey.

For the most part the Montauk fishing scene is about the bigger surf rods and substantial lures. It is the rougher conditions that tend to really get the fish going, and some regular or local anglers will even dress in wetsuits and swim from rock to rock to get at the fish. The first timer would be well advised to head somewhere with a bit more shelter when the sea is up, the fish are running and the striper junkies are out in force, but since Montauk is surrounded on three sides by water you can usually tuck away somewhere. It is a generalisation, but many locals swear by the flood tide on the south side of the peninsula and the ebb or outgoing tide on the north side.

Best times to fish
Striped bass can be caught from the boats from May into October, but shore anglers do best from late May into July and then September through to early November. The spring and the fall runs of bass are what Martha's Vineyard is best known for in saltwater fishing circles

Fishing methods
Lure, bait and fly

Getting there
Easiest way is to get the ferry from Woods Hole to Martha's Vineyard

Tips and tricks
By far and away the best shore fishing for stripers is at night. Go there and become nocturnal

MARTHA'S VINEYARD, USA
Striper fishing is a drug, so think carefully about succumbing to these magnificent striped bass as it could change your life ...

Fishing for striped bass up and down the east and north-east coast of the USA is almost like a religion to those anglers who really do have the striper bug. The striped bass is a true migratory species of fish that moves up and down the east coast according to food sources and seasons. There is a population of stripers on the west coast and even in some landlocked lagoons, but these fish were in fact introduced from the east coast. Striped bass on the east coast actually spawn in freshwater around areas such as the huge Chesapeake Bay system, and then they move up and down the coastline on the hunt for food. There are defined times through the season where they tend to show up strongly in certain areas.

The island of Martha's Vineyard is famous as both a place where the rich and famous go for their summer holidays and also as one of the best destinations to chase big numbers of stripers along with other species such as bluefish, false albacore, bonito and even some bluefin tuna. Situated not far from either New York or Boston, the Vineyard, as it is often known, sits beneath the equally famous Cape Cod area, and at certain times of the year the island is awash with both fish and anglers. There is also the well-known and prestigious annual Martha's Vineyard Striped Bass & Bluefish Derby, where hundreds of anglers can often spend serious time trying to win all manner of prizes. Some anglers will stop work, rent accommodation for the entire derby and literally fish until they drop.

The striped bass tend to arrive in local waters from around the beginning of May, but the fishing really gets going in June and July when the spring migration is at its peak. Shore fishing for stripers drops off somewhat in August as the inshore waters warm up, but then picks up again through September, October and even into November. Boat anglers can usually catch stripers throughout the summer months by looking for areas where the fish are able to find cooler water. The spring run is mostly when the famous 'blitzes' occur – this is when striped bass smash bait close to the surface to create a blitz effect.

Bluefish in particular are huge fun on topwater lures, but you do need a wire trace to deal with their razor sharp teeth. The best times for bluefish from the shore are May and June, but they can and do turn up at almost any time during the striper season. Boat anglers are usually more consistent at finding bluefish into summer and autumn (or fall).

The false albacore is another very popular species that anglers target, especially from late August and on into September. These fish do not hang around in Vineyard waters for that long, but they arrive at the perfect time for many anglers who have satiated their striper addictions and would now prefer some light tackle sport after these blisteringly fast fish.

Best times to fish
Bass fishing is very dependent upon weather and atmospheric pressure. Spring and fall (autumn) are generally the most productive periods of the year in Florida

Fishing methods
Lure, bait and fly

Getting there
Somewhere like Orlando is right at the heart of Florida bass fishing

Tips and tricks
Baitcasting gear is often preferred for helping to set hooks better and then pull the fish out from any structure

FLORIDA, USA
What to some anglers might be their 'everyday' fishing is in fact a whole new experience for a visitor

Most countries have a type of fishing that can perhaps be described as 'typical', and within the USA and the southern states in particular, freshwater bass fishing is just huge. There are even professional bass fishing tournaments and tours, with serious sponsorship participation and prize money. Just as an angler in the UK might go carp fishing on a lake, so the vast majority of freshwater anglers in the USA would look to go freshwater bass fishing. Although the state of Florida is as good a place as any to chase these hard fighting fish, in truth freshwater bass are prevalent throughout much of the warmer southern states. The principal species of bass that are fished for in freshwater are the largemouth and smallmouth, although you could also put the spotted bass in this category. It is the largemouth bass, however, that grows the biggest.

There are any number of well-known lakes within the state of Florida to go bass fishing, with some of the most famous ones being Kissimmee, Okeechobee and Toho. In truth, though, you

do not have to go far to find some quality bass fishing in Florida and, of course, there are any number of saltwater fishing opportunities all around the state. No wonder so many anglers end up visiting Florida at some time or another.

The fact that the US freshwater bass are so inclined to hit both lures and natural baits is perhaps what has afforded them such a popular status amongst anglers. They will often jump when hooked as well, but as much as bass can and do hit artificial and natural baits, like most fish they require a degree of knowledge to catch them consistently. You can, however, find any number of professional bass guides who will take you out fishing throughout the southern USA.

As with any predator, the freshwater bass will tend to look for cover from which they can ambush their prey. The summers get very hot in Florida and, as such, the shallow waters heat up to the point that bass will have to move into deeper water to find more oxygen content. The more cover or vegetation there is to help keep the water cooler, the more the bass can remain in shallower waters. Bass feed on many different species of prey, including shiners (a popular bait) and freshwater crayfish. A substantial amount of US lure fishing owes its advancement to the popularity of bass fishing, with many now accepted techniques and lures having been honed and perfected over the years; the Senko soft plastic worm and Texas rig are but two examples.

Best times to fish
Redfish can be caught all year round, but calm winter days can be particularly rewarding for the big redfish

Fishing methods
Lure, bait and fly

Getting there
Major airports all around this part of the US

Tips and tricks
Redfish are known for fighting really hard, and when releasing them it's important to take time to properly revive the fish

LOUISIANA, USA
The Cajun state is beset with some gloriously remote and pristine marshlands that are often full of redfish

In states such as Florida, Texas, South Carolina and Louisiana there is a species of fish known as the redfish, red drum, red bass or even channel bass, which is targeted up and down the Atlantic and Gulf of Mexico coastlines. Redfish, though, is the most commonly used name for this species. All manner of saltwater fishing takes place in these parts of the world, but Louisiana has some unique aspects that really do help make it one of the must-visit places if you are interested in sight fishing to redfish.

Redfish are a predominantly shallow water fish, and the remote and pristine marshes of Louisiana are such a wonderful contrast to heading miles offshore in search of king mackerel and sailfish, for example. Chasing redfish can also mean year-round fishing; indeed, winter is usually the time when good numbers of big redfish appear in the shallow marshes.

The huge southern Louisiana wetlands are a direct result of all that silt carried by the mighty Mississippi river, and it is perfectly possible to fish for days at a time and never see another vessel

or person. Flats fishing, as it is known, is for the most part all about sight fishing to species such as bonefish, tarpon and permit, but within remote areas like the Louisiana marshlands it's the redfish that is the ultimate flats fish to chase. There is something utterly unique about this fishing, which has any number of anglers completely hooked. In fact, fly fishing for redfish like this is developing all the time. Use some properly balanced fishing tackle and you will see what all the fuss is about.

As much as the redfish are primarily shallow water fish, some of the absolute biggest ones like to hang around the deeper channels that are connected to the open ocean during autumn or fall, hence the reason why they are sometimes referred to as channel bass. Arguably the biggest appeal of fishing for redfish around this part of the US is the opportunity to sight fish to big redfish (often known as bulls) which have come up onto the flats, especially during the calm winter weather. Huge blue skies and flat calm water allow guides and anglers to spot those tell-tale tails finning through the skinny water as the fish forage for food. Spring and early summer is when the brown shrimps start to move back into the marsh ponds and the fishing for numbers of sea trout and redfish really kicks off. Redfish will also take lures and flies off the surface during the warm summer months.

USA

Florida Keys

Best times to fish
There is good fishing all year round in the Keys depending on what you want to target, but the prime times for tarpon are generally mid-March through to July

Fishing methods
Fly, lure and bait

Getting there
Easily accessible from Miami

Tips and tricks
Tarpon love live crabs drifted under the bridges, especially during late evening, night and early morning

THE FLORIDA KEYS, USA
Not for nothing are the Keys on almost every saltwater angler's must-do list

Starting not far south from the sprawling metropolis of Miami, the Florida Keys is a chain of islands that stretches essentially from Key Largo in the north to Key West at its most southerly tip. These islands (or keys) are known the world over as one of the world's premier saltwater fishing destinations; indeed Islamorada is commonly known as the 'Sport Fishing Capital of the World'. The main fishing centres are Key Largo, Islamorada, Marathon, Big Pine Key and the Lower Keys, and Key West.

One of the principal reasons that the Keys are so famous for fishing is that they happen to lie directly in the path of the annual tarpon migration. Whilst some tarpon can be caught year round, it's mainly from about mid-March through to the end of July that sees this incredible concentration of large tarpon using the Keys as a place for mating and spawning. There is no other place on earth that offers such consistent and extensive fishing for one of the world's finest sporting species, from anchoring up and fishing baits under the many road bridges to chasing them over crystal clear sand flats with saltwater fly fishing tackle.

The Florida Keys has one of the largest flats and shallow water ecosystems on earth, which offers fishing for any number of species of fish such as bonefish, permit, snook, redfish, sharks, snappers, grouper, jacks, barracuda, trout, Spanish and cero mackerel, cobia etc. The Keys is perhaps the best place in the world to fly fish for consistently big tarpon, bonefish and, in particular, permit, and all of the islands in the Keys have any number of professional fishing guides with their specialist flats skiffs ready to take you out fishing. There is perhaps no place better set up and organised for sport fishing than the Florida Keys, with a huge selection of hotels, apartments, restaurants, fishing tackle and bait shops, plus caravan/RV parks and boat hire.

However, as much as the Florida Keys quite rightly has such an incredible reputation for its inshore shallow water fishing, do not for one second forget about some truly magical offshore sport as well. On the western side of the Keys you have the shallow waters of the Gulf of Mexico, as well as the massive Everglades system, but on the eastern side of the islands you have the Atlantic Ocean. Heading out into deeper water can at times produce some world class big game fishing for marlin and sailfish to trolled baits and lures, as well as for big dorado, permit on the inshore wrecks in spring, large amberjack, swordfish, massive sharks, jacks, various tuna species, snapper, grouper and, of course, kingfish. There is plenty of easily accessible shore-based fishing throughout the Keys, but this is one area that is almost custom-designed to be fished properly from some kind of boat, and the fishing can be very good all year round for different species.

Best times to fish
There can be good fishing all year round, but the prime times are from February through to June

Fishing methods
Saltwater fly fishing, lure and bait. Principally fly fishing encouraged

Getting there
Direct flights out of Nassau to Inagua

Tips and tricks
Take all the fishing gear you need. No tackle shops on the island at all

GREATER INAGUA, BAHAMAS
Unknown, under-fished, with acres and acres of pristine waters simply full of fish

Closer to Cuba than to Nassau, Greater Inagua, or simply Inagua as it is more commonly known, is a huge and remote Bahamian island that is one of the world's best kept saltwater fly fishing secrets. With no hotels, little meaningful infrastructure, few inhabitants, and about an hour and a half flight away from the sprawling and hectic Nassau, Inagua offers extensive flats systems, a huge inland saltwater lake and a world of potential when it comes to both inshore and offshore fishing. The Bahamas boasts some of the best flats fishing in the world, and Inagua sits there at the pinnacle of what is possible in these extensive and stunning waters. It is the most southerly island in the Bahamas archipelago and the third largest, with an area covering more than 550 square miles.

Ask most saltwater fly fishermen about the Bahamas and they will quite rightly rave about the flats fishing for bonefish; indeed this mercurial fish sits proudly on many of the Bahamian bank notes. Bonefish to the Bahamas are as cigars are to Cuba, and the many islands offer extensive and often untapped areas for chasing these wonderful fish in shallow water. However, there is also a huge amount more to saltwater fly fishing in the Bahamas and Inagua offers a very wide range of fishing. Of course there are plenty of bonefish, and they can sometimes top the magical 10lb mark if you are lucky. But there are also flats and channels that arguably provide some of the best chances in the entire Bahamas for casting flies at large permit, and this on its own makes Inagua seriously special. One of the reasons Inagua is so unique though is that so few fishermen have ever heard about it.

The inland lake is called Lake Windsor and it takes up over one quarter of the interior on its own. Within these often very sheltered waters can be found tarpon, some huge snook, barracuda, bonefish and various snapper species. The tarpon around here do not grow massive, but they can be targeted fairly regularly. The scale of the fishing is hard to comprehend when you think about one single island but, whatever way the wind blows, you can generally find some kind of shelter and fish effectively on both the flats or Lake Windsor.

However, fishing as remote and as good as this is not as easy to access as say a salmon lodge on the banks of a Norwegian spate river. There is only one professional fishing guide on Inagua and virtually all his clients stay in his cottages next door. You are bound by what are at times some mildly erratic flight schedules, so it is advisable to organise a couple of 'safety' days either side of your trip somewhere around Nassau. And don't forget that there are many lifetimes of Bahamian flats systems to explore throughout the vast archipelago. Inagua is but one island of the Bahamas, yet it offers some of the most remote and unspoilt saltwater fishing you can find.

USA

Mexico | Caribbean Sea

Campeche

Pacific Ocean

Best times to fish
All year, but the hottest summer months can be especially good

Fishing methods
Fly fishing

Getting there
Generally accessed from Merida International Airport

Tips and tricks
Mostly floating line fishing, but it is worth taking a sinking line to get down in the deeper channels

CAMPECHE, MEXICO

Hordes of baby tarpon rolling in gin clear water within a fascinating UNESCO World Heritage site

Within the huge marine reserve of Los Petenes, on the west side of Mexico's Yucatan peninsula, there is a fascinating saltwater fishery that revolves around fishing for big numbers of small to medium-sized tarpon. Indeed, this location is becoming increasingly well known for just that. There are a few well-documented parts of the world where you might choose to go and fish for big to potentially huge tarpon, but the fishing around Campeche in Mexico is all about having an enormous amount of fun on the year-round, resident shoals of smaller tarpon that abound.

There are over 80 miles of coastline perfectly suited to this 'baby' tarpon fishing, with numerous mangroves, creeks, channels and flats to fish around. Where your guide takes you fishing is mainly down to the weather conditions and wind direction, but with all that terrain and potential shelter, the odds are hugely stacked in your favour to come across large numbers of 'baby' tarpon willing to eat your fly. There are also species such as snook and jack crevalle to fish for.

The water is generally gin clear, and whatever the size of tarpon charging down your fly there are few things like it in saltwater fishing. For the most part the tarpon are around 5-40lbs in weight. The fishing days in the main start early, and your guide will be looking for tarpon rolling on the surface, a sight that alone should be enough to set your heart racing. Rolling tarpon on the flats usually happens when there is virtually no wind, but if a breeze is blowing then the clear water allows you to head into the mangroves, inlets and channels to sight fish for cruising tarpon in the slightly deeper water.

Tarpon are tarpon, whether they are 'babies' or 'monsters', and this Campeche fishery is seeing all kinds of saltwater fly fishing junkies making the easy trek here. From beginner to seasoned pro, getting multiple shots at hungry tarpon each day is what is making this place increasingly appealing, but with that much water around there is little chance of any overcrowding.

It is simply great saltwater fly fishing to be able to use, for example, 7 weight fly rods out on the flats on a calm day, but step up to an 8 or even 9 weight outfit if the wind is up and you need to punch lines out or if there are some pods of larger fish around. This is a fishery that is only just beginning to be really explored and understood, but it is without doubt one of the most prolific fledgling tarpon fisheries there is.

Atlantic Ocean

Cuba

Jardines de
la Reina

Caribbean Sea

Best times to fish
The period of October through to August tends to offer the best fishing and weather

Fishing methods
Mainly fly fishing, but also some lure and bait fishing

Getting there
Many airlines fly to Havana in Cuba, and then your fishing operator will take over from there and get you to your mothership and the fishing

Tips and tricks
As much as the bones, permit and tarpon are of course the main attraction, don't ignore the various snappers and jacks

JARDINES DE LA REINA, CUBA
You don't need flowers to have a perfectly magical garden

The Jardines de la Reina (the Queen's Gardens) is an immaculately pristine chain of islands that lies off the coast of south-east Cuba and stretches for more than 100 miles. There is no commercial fishing pressure in these waters; indeed they have been designated a Cuban National Park. As with the Florida Keys, the Jardines de la Reina is a huge series of islands and flats, and its remoteness helps to protect what is one of the finest saltwater fisheries in the world. Much of it is many miles offshore and therefore the fishing operations are run exclusively from motherships.

Again, similar to the Florida Keys, the Jardines de la Reina offers some truly outstanding saltwater fly fishing for permit, bonefish and tarpon, although it does not have the sheer numbers of very large migratory tarpon that you can come across at the Keys. However, rest assured that at the right time of year there are enough big tarpon moving through to keep any angler in a constant state of nervous exhaustion. The Florida Keys is a truly world class fishery, but you will of course find a substantial lack of people and boats on these remote Cuban islands.

There is arguably no saltwater fish that is better suited to fly fishing than the bonefish, and the pristine, quiet flats that abound around Jardines de la Reina can lay claim to some of the best bonefishing ever. The waters are literally crawling with bonefish of around 4-6lbs, but there are not too many places on earth that can offer such consistent shots at really big 10lb plus bonefish. Some of the fishing will be via wading, while some will be from skiffs. The general lack of pressure on these fish really gives the angler some great chances at good numbers of large fish, but on the flip side you can at times have to cover a lot of water to find bones like that. Little is ever going to beat the sight of tailing bonefish on a shimmering sand flat as the light just begins to fade.

The Jardines de la Reina needs to be on your list if you fancy the chance of catching big permit on the flats. Grand slams are always a distinct possibility in these waters and some of the permit are impressively large. There are plenty of 'baby' tarpon in the 20-50lb class, but from about March to June there is an influx of larger fish that can easily go over 100lbs. You can also catch some really big jacks, which will pull serious string in the shallow water, and for a wind down you can even go and get your lures or baits ripped to pieces on the reefs and in the channels. Species like cubera and mutton snappers, barracuda and groupers abound.

Best times to fish
There is some good fishing all year round, but February to the end of September offers you the most consistent conditions for sight fishing. There is a hurricane season between June and November, but this does not actually mean that there will be any. July and August can actually be particularly good times for the flats fishing

Fishing methods
Mainly fly fishing

Getting there
Fly in to Cancun and then use the road or air connections to where you will be staying

Tips and tricks
Keep an eye out at all times on the channels and cuts between the flats for species like jacks and barracuda. Hugely fun fish on fly gear

YUCATAN PENINSULA, MEXICO
Without doubt one of the best areas to go and chase permit on the flats. Don't let them get you down though

There is a wealth of fishing opportunities around Mexico's Yucatan peninsula, and whilst a few places have sadly become somewhat over-developed tourist traps, it is not at all hard to get off the beaten track and find some very good fishing. The whole area is especially famous for the inshore and flats-based saltwater fly fishing. Campeche is becoming increasingly well known for its hugely fun 'baby tarpon' fishing, but then also look at areas such as Ascension Bay, Boca Paila, Espiritu Santo Bay and Chetumal Bay in the south. The whole crux of the wonderful inshore fishing around the Yucatan is the direct access that these waters have to the Caribbean Sea and species such as tarpon, bonefish, permit and snook, which thrive in the shallow habitats.

Permit on the flats are arguably the ultimate shallow water species, and dedicated anglers (perhaps junkies might be a better term) can and do spend extraordinary amounts of time and effort on the hunt for them. Few species of fish, however, can drive an angler to such distraction with their extremely finicky nature and their ordinarily flat refusal to eat a perfectly well presented fly. But when that permit does take, it makes all the heartache worthwhile, and parts of the Yucatan peninsula offer some fantastic permit fishing when conditions are favourable. Just seeing those tell-tale black tales waving in the breeze as a permit is head down and happily feeding away is enough to bring about some quite extraordinary reactions amongst saltwater anglers, and places like Ascension Bay are famous the world over for the chance to complete the saltwater grand slam. A bonefish, permit and tarpon in one day is about as good as it gets, and you might even get a shot at the Super Grand Slam if you can add a snook to that exclusive list of fish.

The massive Ascension Bay or Bahia de l'Ascension gives anglers easy access to many, many square miles of sandy beaches, lagoons, shallow bays and, of course, almost too many flats to fully comprehend. Much of the fishing is done by wading the shallow waters. From May to September you can chase larger migratory tarpon around Isla Holbox, on the northern coastline of the Yucatan peninsula, and of course, like at Campeche, there are many small to medium tarpon present all year round. If you want to access some good fishing not far from the bustling Cancun, then you should look around for guides who operate in the Chacmuchuk Lagoon close to Isla Blanca. Most of the fishing will be done from a boat as the flats are not so easy to wade as in Ascension Bay.

Cuba

Mexico

Central America

Caribbean Sea

Rio Parismina

Costa Rica

Pacific Ocean

Best times to fish
Good fishing at most times, apart from after heavy rains and the resulting high waters in June/July and from November to January

Fishing methods
Bait, lure and fly

Getting there
San Jose airport provides good access to Costa Rica's Caribbean coastline

Tips and tricks
Make sure you go and do some of the freshwater fishing. Not only is the fishing excellent, but most of it is done within the magnificent Tortuguero National Park. The rainforest is pristine

RIO PARISMINA, COSTA RICA, CENTRAL AMERICA
Silver kings abound in these warm Central American waters

The Parismina river (or Rio Parismina) is situated along the Caribbean coastline of Costa Rica. As well as providing some very good tarpon fishing within the network of lagoons, rivers, beaches and open ocean, this area also offers plenty of fishing for very big snook. It is possible to fly fish for the tarpon, but in essence this is a very prolific tarpon fishery that is best targeted with bait and lure fishing tackle. For the most part, the best of the tarpon fishing happens along the coastline at depths which essentially take sight fishing with fly gear out of the equation, although you can of course sometimes fish successfully with fast sinking lines and big weighted flies. However, with tarpon or 'silver kings', as they are often known being one of the world's finest sporting fish, there are any number of saltwater anglers who want to tangle with them via a range of different methods. The Rio Parismina area is home to a significant quantity of tarpon in the 50-100lb range, with plenty of larger fish up to around 150lbs at times. On any gear a tarpon is one serious fish to deal with, so don't worry too much about how you might fish for them, but instead hang on tightly as they jump repeatedly and generally do all they can to upset your wellbeing.

Because the Rio Parismina is such a prolific fishery, particularly on bait gear, the first-time tarpon angler might well consider coming here to break his duck and mess with some challenging fish. If sight fishing to these silver kings is the only way you want to fish for them though, then you would need to go elsewhere to places such as the Keys, Belize, Cuba and Mexico. Throughout the Rio Parismina area, the tarpon seem to show a marked preference for lurking around the discoloured waters at the mouths of the rivers. The boat skippers will tend to look for rolling fish and then motor uptide of them to drop baits back. Fly anglers do fish here and can do well if they are prepared to get down to the feeding tarpon.

The snook fishing is usually best in the river mouth, but in truth there are endless fishing options outside of the excellent tarpon fishing. Snook to world record sizes have been caught around the Rio Parismina, and you can also find them in the lagoons and rivers. Snook will respond well to lures on lighter tackle, but never for one second think that these fish are a pushover. There is also some fun fishing right up the rivers in the jungle for species such as guapote, machaca, mojarra, four different species of snook, tarpon and mangrove snappers. If your arms have been well and truly harmed by hordes of tarpon but you are up for a bit more pain, then think about messing with jacks, king mackerel, wahoo and tuna just a few miles offshore.

Best times to fish
A long season,
February to October

Fishing methods
Saltwater fly fishing

Getting there
Flights from Caracas
in Venezuela

Tips and tricks
Make sure to take a look
around the pier early in
the mornings and cast
Gummy Minnow flies at
the massive bonefish

LOS ROQUES ARCHIPELAGO, VENEZUELA
Serious numbers of bonefish creeping onto pristine flats as far as the eye can see

The Los Roques archipelago lies 85 miles off the coast of Venezuela and offers some of the world's finest and most consistent fly fishing for bonefish on the miles and miles of pristine shallow water sand flats. The saltwater fly fishing community first stumbled upon this perfect location only back in the mid-1980s and, since then, it has become some kind of mecca for quality bonefishing. What makes this place so special is that there is no commercial fishing at all allowed within this national park, and even then there are large areas that are off-limits to sport anglers. All sport fishing is licensed and regulated so that the extensive flats do not receive too much pressure from anglers, and with such high numbers of large average-sized bonefish, Los Roques has become established as one of the must-visit saltwater fly fishing destinations.

The archipelago is very easy to get to, with regular flights in and out of Caracas airport in Venezuela. Due to its proximity to the equator, the archipelago enjoys extended periods of stable weather and warm consistent temperatures, with very little rain.

Within the fishing area of the national park lie masses of islands of different sizes, and surrounding most of these are a multitude of shallow water sand flats. Los Roques is a wade fishery, in that your guide will take you to the fishing area on a boat, but after that you are wading these sublimely shallow waters. This is a big part of what makes Los Roques so special; there is no fishing allowed without the use of a registered professional guide.

Los Roques is also one of those rare 'hardcore' fishing destinations that are perfect for non-fishing partners and families. Within this marine park you can do activities such as snorkelling, diving and wind surfing, as well as simply spend time wandering around the town and surrounding area. There are no cars on the archipelago.

One of the reasons why Los Roques is such a must-visit bonefish location is the length of the fishing season. There will be significant numbers of bonefish up on the flats usually from February to October, and even in the summer months the place is more than fishable with the cooling trade winds. As well as bonefish, you stand a chance of fishing to permit, tarpon and jacks, with the town's pier being home to a pretty unique spectacle where some truly monster bonefish prey on the vast shoals of minnows. Pelicans are of course a part of this feeding frenzy, and the big localised bonefish have developed a way of knocking minnows out of a pelican's beak and then hoovering them up. An easy meal you might say. Some big tarpon also swim around this pier, but landing them with the boat traffic and mooring ropes around is not remotely easy.

Best times to fish
Best fishing for sailfish is
October through to May

Fishing methods
Lures, bait and fly fishing

Getting there
Easily accessible out of
somewhere like Miami or
Madrid in Europe

Tips and tricks
Learn how to strip strike
a fly rod when a big fish
is eating your fly. It can
take great self-control
when your heart is
pumping though

GUATEMALA, CENTRAL AMERICA
**Arguably the most consistent sailfish fishery there is,
with multiple shots per day an ever-present possibility**

The Pacific coastline of Guatemala is an incredibly fish-rich waterway, with vast
numbers of baitfish and larger pelagic species. The coast essentially forms one giant
bay that funnels the currents into producing a kind of massive natural eddy into which
the predators come to feed hard upon the smaller bait species. Guatemala offers some
excellent all-round saltwater fishing, but as a fishery it is undoubtedly best known for the
incredibly consistent levels of Pacific sailfish fishing. This is the place to go if you want to
catch these fast-swimming fish, especially on the fly. There is very little commercial fishing
pressure in these warm waters, and besides the Pacific sailfish, you might also get to catch
mahi mahi, tuna and marlin offshore as well as jacks and the highly sought-after rooster
fish closer inshore.

It is possible to catch sailfish virtually all year round off Guatemala if conditions remain
favourable, and within the absolute prime times of October to the end of May there is an
incredible average of around 15-20 shots at feeding sailfish each day. The average size
of these Pacific sailfish is around 80lbs, but 100lb plus fish are not remotely uncommon.
The best professional sport fishing boats will be releasing around 2,000 sailfish each
year, and the marlin fishing seems to be getting increasingly better too, especially from
early summer into autumn (fall). It is generally recognised that the waters off the coast of
Guatemala are the most prolific sailfish breeding grounds in the world.

The most accepted way to fish for sailfish is by trolling baits and lures, but fly fishing
for them is becoming progressively popular. In essence the boat must still troll hookless
lures or baits to draw the sailfish in, and then it becomes a skilful combination of skipper,
deckhand and angler. Relatively heavy fly fishing tackle has to be used to tame these
insanely fast fish, and the casting of heavy flies and lines is somewhat restricted from a
pitching boat. But it can and does work incredibly well. It is vital that a hungry sailfish is
literally teased in close to the boat where the fly angler can then have a chance at
putting the fly down in front of the chasing fish. The speed at which a hooked sailfish
can hit a fly and then suddenly be more than 100 yards away, repeatedly jumping clear
of the water, more often than not reduces the first-timer to a quivering wreck. The sailfish
fishery is operated under a strict catch and release policy to help ensure the future of
this amazing sport.

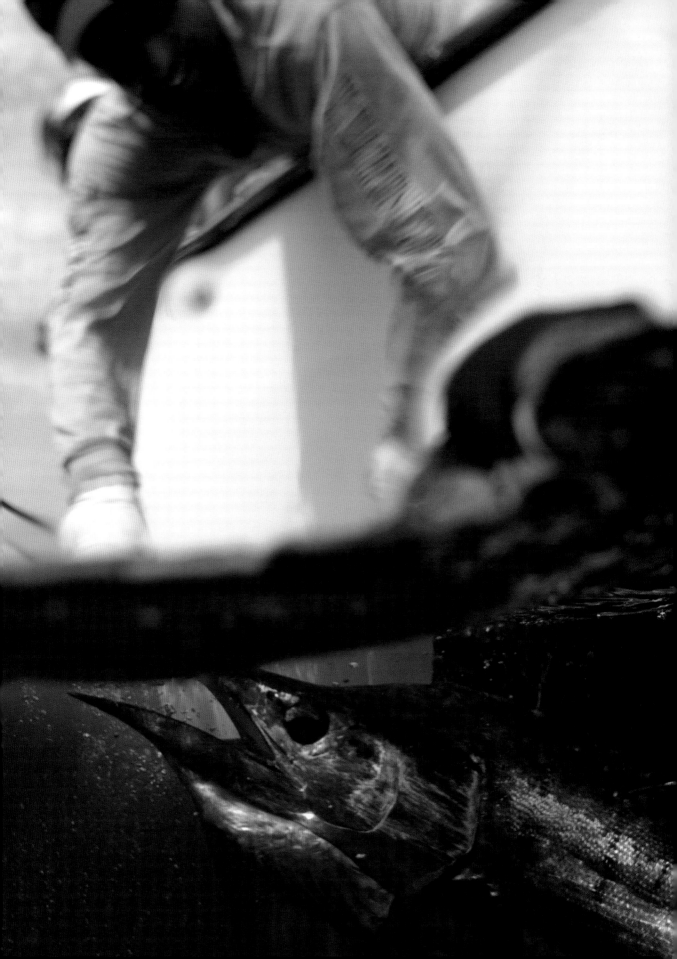

AMBERGRIS CAYE, BELIZE
Tarpon, tarpon everywhere. Plus an abundance of permit and bonefish. Heaven on earth?

Best times to fish
There is fishing all year round, with the most settled times being around April to September. The biggest tarpon are migrating through from July to September

Fishing methods
Depends on where you stay. Some lodges like fly only, but some are keen on lures and bait as well

Getting there
Belize international airport and then generally a short flight to the local town of San Pedro

Tips and tricks
If you are up for it, do your guided day's fishing, come back to the lodge, and then jump in a kayak and head off to fish the backcountry for bonefish and perhaps snook

There are few better places to really stand a good chance of nailing fly fishing's 'grand slam', or in plain English, catching a bonefish, permit and tarpon in one day. Outside of the huge Florida Keys flats system, the shallow water so prevalent close inshore around much of Belize is perhaps the next most consistent area to go and chase tarpon, and these mighty fish patrol the warm waters all year round. The Ambergris Caye fishery is huge, around some 250 square miles, and it boasts year round resident tarpon of up to perhaps 100lbs. But one of the real pulls of saltwater fly fishing in Belize is that it is on the migratory path of even more tarpon, and these bigger fish move through during July, August and September.

The main reason that this extensive area offers such good conditions for saltwater fly fishing is the vast, 190-mile long coral reef that runs down the coast less than a mile offshore. This living reef is the second largest coral reef in the world, and what it does is help bring about very sheltered conditions inside of the reef for fly fishing. Ambergris Caye itself is around 25 miles long and over a mile wide in some places.

What Belize tends to lack in size of bonefish, it more than makes up for in numbers of fish on the flats, and most of the bones run in the 2-5lb mark. Many of the flats are wadeable, and you can even take kayaks from somewhere like the famous El Pescador lodge and go into the backcountry lagoons looking for fish. For the most part, the guided fishing around here is done from the local and traditional 23-foot panga boats, which have casting and poling platforms for clients and guides alike.

Large schools of permit are often found on the bonefish and tarpon flats, and whilst the average size is around 8-10lbs, they have been caught up to around 30lbs. Note though that any Atlantic permit caught on the flats on fly gear is a serious achievement as it is. When those telltale black tails are seen almost flapping in the breeze as the fish feed head down, it is not at all uncommon for the visiting angler to get so excited that their general fishing abilities go into complete meltdown for a while. Permit on the flats tend to do that to people.

As well as the principal three flats-based species, you can also find some big snook hiding in the mangroves on the flats, and in the deep water channels between most flats there are often large shoals of very hungry and wonderfully aggressive jacks, which love to munch flies.

Best times to fish
October to April, but rains can occur at almost any time and could affect the fishing. This is the Amazon basin

Fishing methods
Fly fishing only

Getting there
Lodge is accessed from Manaus in Brazil

Tips and tricks
Use the best polarised sunglasses you can lay your hands on, and then take a spare pair for a remote trip like this. There are no tackle shops out in the middle of the jungle

RORAIMA STATE, AMAZON BASIN, BRAZIL
Get your arms pulled in true style deep within the Amazon rainforest

The immense Amazon basin boasts the largest freshwater river system on earth. Within the northern part of the state of Roraima lies the Rio Agua Boa, a unique tributary of the Rio Branco, which is in turn a confluent of the Rio Negro, a vast tributary of the Amazon. The Rio Agua Boa is very special in that at certain times of the year its waters run clear, and this gives rise to some true rainforest-based fly fishing for one of the most amazing looking freshwater species there is. Sight fishing to peacock bass is among freshwater fly fishing's ultimate 'to do's'.

There are various species of peacock bass, and in the main they are fish with explosive energy that will do everything within their considerable power to reach any kind of sanctuary. The remote Agua Boa fishing lodge is a fly fishing only operation that sits on the banks of the clear Rio Agua Boa. This incredible area of the Amazon rainforest is heavily protected via the Brazilian Environmental Institute. Absolutely no commercial fishing is allowed in this region, and the sport fishing is a strict catch and release operation.

Although there are plenty of the smaller butterfly peacock bass around, visiting anglers are primarily going to be targeting the much larger three-bar peacock bass which have been caught up to nearly 30lbs. When a fish like this hits and then jumps repeatedly, it's often a case of hold on as hard as you can and hope that things go your way. There are some who consider the peacock bass to be the hardest fighting freshwater species in the world, but of course anglers who have tangled with the insane Papua New Guinea black bass might disagree. Whatever the truth, a big peacock bass is going to hit you and strip you to the backing, usually without you being able to do a single thing about it. This kind of jungle fly fishing is about as far removed from the gentle art of deftly fishing a dry fly on a chalkstream in southern England, for example, but then variety is what makes this sport so appealing.

As well as the peacock bass, there are a number of other species of fish that you might end up catching. The days of trout and salmon being virtually the only freshwater species fished for on fly gear are long gone. In the clear waters of the Rio Agua Boa you could see fish such as the arowana, pacu, matrincha and pirarucu.

Best times to fish
January to the end
of March

Fishing methods
Lure, bait and fly

Getting there
Out of Manaus in Brazil

Tips and tricks
If you are going to go
somewhere as far away
and remote as this, take
the absolute best fishing
tackle you can afford

RIO URARIQUERA, SOUTH AMERICA

Many fish you will have never heard of are ready and waiting deep within the Amazon rainforest

Deep within the northern fringes of the vast Amazon basin lies the 75-mile long Maraca Island, which sits on the Rio Urariquera. This huge and pristine ecosystem has for many years been completely closed off to fishing, but it is now possible for a limited time each year to gain access to these waters via some strict regulations that limit the impact sport fishing can have on this important part of Brazil. The fish species tend to be so large and the waters so pristine that the Brazilian government is even helping to facilitate some US universities to study these waterways. The Ilha de Maraca reserve is home to unquestionably some of the most diverse and tackle-crunching freshwater fishing that there is, but it takes some serious logistical expertise from the people on the ground to safely put anglers onto these remote waters.

An incredibly divergent array of waterfalls, rapids and fast currents exist within the stretches of river that are fished, and the species that can be caught are just so far removed from the norm that you simply never know what might hit your lure, fly or bait. There is a high chance that it will be large, have big teeth and want to take plenty of line very quickly.

As Africa has the mad-looking tigerfish, so the Amazon has the paraya. These brutal predators are an incredibly exciting fish to catch, and on the Rio Urariquera they can sometimes be caught in large numbers, often to over 20lbs. These fish fight extremely hard and will make multiple head-shaking jumps. During the dry season they migrate up-river as they follow the shoals of baitfish, and this unique river has various areas that offer good reason for predators like these to hang around and feed. If the baitfish are there then you should find good numbers of paraya.

There is also a high volume of pirapitinga, or pacu, as they are more commonly known. Like the paraya, they are hard fighting fish that can often weigh over the 20lb mark. If you like weird and wonderful catfish then the waters of the Amazon are a good place to go, and within the Rio Urariquera there are species such as the huge, potentially 300lb plus piraiba, the possibly 200lb plus jaru, the red-tailed catfish as well as almost who knows what else. Words are not enough to do justice to the sheer variety of fish that swim in these remote rivers. How about catching piranha? How about species such as bicuda, yatorana, jundira and pescada? Most anglers have never even heard of fish like this let alone fished for them.

Best times to fish
May until mid-October

Fishing methods
Fly fishing only, although you can fish for the large catfish with bait

Getting there
Local flights run out of Santa Cruz

Tips and tricks
Felt-soled wading boots offer the best grip when wet-wading the river. They are absolutely vital

JUNGLE RIVERS, BOLIVIA
Unrelenting savagery deep within distant South American jungles

Deep within the mass of remote Bolivian jungle lie some incredibly special rivers where one of the world's greatest and most savage freshwater species of fish plies its trade. As trout are iconic to English fly fishermen, so the magnificent golden dorado is one of South America's most coveted freshwater species to fish for on fly, lure and bait. As much as these bars of gold are widespread through large tracts of South America, the hunt is always on for intimate rivers where you can sight fish in clear waters. Some of the remote rivers of the Bolivian jungle offer what is arguably among the finest, wildest and purest freshwater fishing on this planet. Sight fishing of gold coloured predators in warm jungle rivers is about as good as any kind of fishing gets.

The finest fishing would not be what it is if it were easy to access, and getting to these few rivers, which the local population have granted selected fishing rights on, requires a flight deep into the heart of wild jungle and then various boat rides up or down some winding waterways. Rustic but comfortable fishing lodges have been built overlooking a couple of the rivers that are fished. The Itirizama river offers the most genuine sight fishing opportunities for the golden dorado and also for some very large Amazon pacu, which almost haunt some of the larger pools further upstream. They have been likened to freshwater permit.

Golden dorado are out and out predators, and in these remote jungle rivers they rely on the numerous shoals of unfortunate sabalo that are their principal diet. What is so unique about these rivers is that they are essentially flushed out each year with the seasonal rains. The principal fish species all head way downstream and then begin to return, almost like migratory salmon, as the river levels drop. First come the shoals of sabalo, upon which the local people rely, and these fish are then followed by the predatory golden dorado.

The different parts of the rivers are usually accessed via narrow canoes and boats, but for the most part the fly fishing is done from the bank or via wet-wading out in the warm waters. When the river becomes impossible to navigate with the boats, you get out and walk. There is no denying the fact that at times it can be a very physical form of fly fishing if you want to access some of the even more remote upstream pools and runs, but the effort required is more than worth it when you see big dorado smashing into shoals of sabalo like giant trevally (GTs) might do on the saltwater flats. To see a dorado charging down your fly like a rabid dog is some very unique freshwater fly fishing indeed.

Best times to fish
Nearly year round, but the boats are out of the water in June and July when it is too cold for good fishing

Fishing methods
Fly and lure

Getting there
Either a private charter flight out of Buenos Aires, or otherwise about a six hour journey by road

Tips and tricks
Strong hooks absolutely vital. Change all hooks on your lures for better and stronger ones

LA ZONA, ARGENTINA
Industrial-sized golden predators with appetites to match

Not by any means a pretty or scenic place to fish, yet the La Zona region of the Uruguay river, just below the somewhat austere looking Salto Grande dam, is without doubt home to the largest golden dorado in the world. It is only since 2004 that any sportfishing has been allowed below the dam, and even then it is very tightly controlled to help protect these monster fish. There is only one lodge that has access to the fishing at La Zona. Gradually these mighty fish are becoming more and more known about outside of South America, and the famous US fly fisherman, Larry Dahlberg, was moved to call the golden dorado 'the world's toughest game fish'. Praise indeed. There is nowhere else known about where the chance of taking a 40lb plus golden dorado is more likely, and La Zona now holds numerous International Game Fish Association (IGFA) records for this species.

You are allowed to fish for the golden dorado at La Zona with either fly or lure fishing tackle. Indeed it could be argued that the local guides have to be some of the most knowledgeable people there are when it comes to fly fishing for these particular fish. Wire traces are essential to either fly or lure to counteract the viciously sharp teeth, and it is not uncommon to hook a smaller dorado and then have it unceremoniously attacked by a somewhat larger specimen. At times you can see dorado hitting shoals of bait fish near the surface, much as a shoal of jacks might do in the open ocean, and it is all you can do to remind yourself that this is actually freshwater fishing.

The fishing is only a few hours' drive north of Buenos Aires, or you can just as easily fly here. The lodge is situated immediately downstream of the actual fishing area, and the fishing is tightly regulated and controlled. No more than four anglers per week can fish La Zona, which works out at two anglers to a boat, with one or two guides per boat. Although the fish are present year round, there are of course prime times when the water flows coming from the dam tend to be more consistent. The period from January to April generally offers the best fishing, and you are always in with a chance of taking big golden dorado off the surface on lures or flies. Make sure to change all treble hooks on your lures for stronger models, as these fish show no respect to anything they decide to eat. Golden dorado jump repeatedly when hooked, so be prepared and do not give slack line to the fish when this happens.

Argentina

Atlantic
Ocean

Pacific
Ocean

Rio Gallegos

Best times to fish
The season starts just
after Christmas and runs
to around mid-April

Fishing methods
Fly fishing

Getting there
Most connections to this
remote part of the world
will depart out of Buenos
Aires in Argentina

Tips and tricks
Take the best waders,
wading boots, wading
jacket and layering
system you can afford.
This will be money
seriously well spent

RIO GALLEGOS, ARGENTINA
Cut your fly through the howling winds and out across a river stuffed full of monster sea trout

The Rio Gallegos is one of the most famous rivers on earth when it comes to chasing exceptionally large sea trout, or sea run browns as they are sometimes known. The river starts in the southern Andes as the Penitente and the Ruebens and runs for close to 200 miles until it empties into the sea. The other main sea trout river is the Rio Grande, and together these two rivers only started to produce sea trout because of the introduction of brown trout in 1935. For some reason these rivers yield almost abnormally large sea trout of an average size that almost defies belief. It is not an exaggeration to say that the average size of sea trout on the Rio Grande is around 12lbs, and plenty of fish are taken over the 20lb mark.

These rivers are situated almost at the bottom of the fly fishing world, and this narrow strip of Argentina means that there is frequently a strong westerly wind blowing in from the ocean. But as much as it can sometimes be fairly tricky bracing yourself against this constant barrage, more often than not the wind whistles down the river and can actually aid with your casting. The fact

that the surface of the water is usually so ruffled is perhaps a reason why these sea trout are so readily caught during daylight hours.

Many of the named pools along the Rio Gallegos can be fished successfully with a single-handed fly rod, but there will be times when a double-hander comes in more than useful for combating the wind and launching the larger flies out there. The more turbulent and stirred up the water is, the larger the flies should be to pick out any number of these hugely aggressive sea trout. Clearer, calmer water calls for a more subtle approach with smaller fly patterns. The southern hemisphere's summer is the best time for this sea trout fishing, and for the most part it is fairly dry. This is important in order to retain as much clarity in the main river as possible, although it does usually clear fairly quickly after any heavy rain.

The sea trout tend to be caught via a mixture of more traditional Atlantic salmon style methods, where you cast out across the river and then allow the fly to swing in the current, and stripping the smaller flies through the various features of the river such as seams and tails. For many anglers this is one of the true pinnacles of freshwater fly fishing anywhere on earth, but there is no getting away from the fact that it is an enormous trek to get here. The best fishing, though, is often far from the beaten track. Do not for one second scrimp on any fishing gear or clothing when you travel that far to fish.

Best times to fish
Generally from mid-November to mid-March

Fishing methods
Fly fishing

Getting there
Most connections to this part of South America leave out of Buenos Aires in Argentina

Tips and tricks
Make sure you pick your jaw up off the floor as you come across those stunning landscapes

PATAGONIA, CHILE
Jaw-droppingly stunning trout fishing at the bottom of the world

If freshwater fishing around the more upper parts of South America revolves largely around the quite magical golden dorado, then the region known as Patagonia is predominantly about world class trout fishing in the numerous rivers and lakes that are fed from the mighty Andes. Patagonia is a region essentially straddling the southern end of South America, and it stretches across large parts of both Chile and Argentina. From the more adventurous tourist point of view, it would have to be the wild and rugged Torres del Paine National Park that Patagonia is most well-known for, but for fly fishermen it's the quality of the brown and rainbow trout fishing that brings them here. Fly fishing in Patagonia is a real opportunity to spend time in a true wilderness where the only things you see might well be condors and eagles wheeling about overhead. Trout are not native to Chile or Argentina, but they have thrived after their introduction in the mid-1800s. As well as brown and rainbow trout, in different areas you can also catch brook trout, various salmon species, as well as of course some huge sea trout (sea run browns) and even steelhead (sea run rainbows).

The Lakes District is beset with numerous large and very clear lakes that are in turn connected by any number of gin-clear rivers. It almost goes without saying that this area, which lies beneath the majestic Andes, is a trout fishing heaven. Trout grow especially big here, partly due to the presence of a small freshwater crab called the Pancora crab. If the trout are not rising to hatching flies then there is every chance they are gorging on this natural food source on the bottom. Fishing here surrounded by snow capped mountains, temperate rain forests and a serious lack of people is what Patagonia fly fishing is all about. The rivers in the Lakes District run mainly clear during the trout season because they are fed by rain and not by snow melt.

The remote and virtually uninhabited area known as the Chilean Fjords dictate that most access for the fly fishing has to be done by water. Around 1,000 miles of lakes and rivers stretch from Puerto Montt to Punta Arenas, with a range of mountains close to the coast providing plenty of changeable weather patterns. Many of the rivers hold both rainbow and brown trout, while in a few you can even catch a king (Pacific) salmon. Fly anglers travelling to this isolated part of the world will generally have one thing on their mind and that is some potentially huge browns and rainbows. Anywhere where the brown trout tend to average around 5lbs is going to get the heart racing, especially when fishing amongst such striking scenery.

Greenland
Sea

**Laxa I Adaldal
river**
Iceland

Atlantic Ocean

Best times to fish
Late June and July are
the best times for the
trout fishing

Fishing methods
Fly fishing

Getting there
Either a long drive
from Keflavik airport or
otherwise connect in
from Akureyri airport
further north

Tips and tricks
You need to dress for any
kind of weather, from
really hot to very cold

LAXA I ADALDAL RIVER, ICELAND
The land of fire and ice is not just about
world class salmon fishing

As much as Iceland is an internationally renowned Atlantic salmon fishing destination,
with its plethora of rivers and streams, it also has some far less known about but possibly as
equally world class wild brown trout fishing. On a river such as the Laxa I Adaldal, in the north
of Iceland, there is every possibility of connecting with a 10lb plus wild brown, with numerous fish
in the 5–7lb class. Sometimes it can be hard on a river like this to know whether to chase the
salmon or the trout.

Although the Laxa I Adaldal is also a prime salmon river, there are two main beats where the
trout fishing is utterly fantastic. The Laxardal and Myvatnssveit beats together offer over 20 miles
of prime fly fishing for trout.

Due to the country's weather patterns, the Icelandic trout have a short season to really feed
up on the various insect hatches that take place during the warmer months, so if you find the fish
are on, then you might be in for a truly magical day's fly fishing. Considering that a few wild brown

trout over the 12lb mark have been taken from this river, you always need to be prepared for the sheer size of fish you might suddenly connect with.

In places the river does not look very clear, but this is because the bottom is often made up of dark coloured sand that then gives the impression of murkiness. The trout are as wary and as clever as they are in any other clear running river, so for the most part the use of small flies and stealthy approach tactics will pay dividends. Although fishing downstream with streamers might well be one of the favoured local tactics, generally you are going to have more success by fishing using upstream dry fly and nymph methods as per on the southern English chalkstreams, for example. These wild Icelandic trout are incredibly strong, so you want to think about stepping up a gear as regards tackle.

Few other countries are so well geared up for sport fishing, and Iceland is beset with any number of comfortable fishing lodges to cater for visitors who come from all around the world. There are a number of external fishing trip operators offering different parts of Iceland for fly fishing, but if you want to experience some of the best trout fishing going, then make sure you look up a company that lists the sublime Laxa I Adaldal on its books. Go prepared for any kind of weather, from very warm to close to freezing in the same day, and near 24 hour daylight during the mid-summer months can make for some very long fishing days.

Best times to fish
Exact seasons vary from
river to river, but the best
of the salmon fishing on
these two rivers tends to
be around July onwards

Fishing methods
Fly fishing

Getting there
Reykjavik is easily
reached from many
international airports

Tips and tricks
Wear layered clothing
and prepare for big
temperature fluctuations

WEST COAST SALMON RIVERS, ICELAND

The land of fire and ice is home to some of the best Atlantic salmon fishing in the world

Iceland has almost a ridiculous number of rivers that run with Atlantic salmon, to the point that travelling around this wonderfully diverse country might seem a little overwhelming or even daunting if you are one of those anglers who cannot look at a bit of water without getting excited about what might swim within. Most anglers, of course, fall into that category, and with that in mind it might be worth thinking about the west coast of Iceland to narrow things down a little, and specifically the Langá and the Nordura. With the right conditions, these can be hugely prolific salmon rivers, and due to Iceland being so easily accessible and these two rivers being close to each other, you are able to maximise your fishing time and make use of the long daylight hours during the summer months.

The Langá is only 22 miles long, but within that short length it has 93 named salmon pools. Despite its lack of size, this interesting waterway offers some technical fly fishing with smaller rods amongst some truly wonderful Icelandic backdrops. One of the most famous and heart-stopping ways to fish for salmon in many of the Icelandic rivers is to work with these single-handed rods and cast small, hitched-style flies out across the water and then let them swing around in the current. Imagine a salmon hitting a fly off the top. The salmon fishing in Iceland is very well managed and looked after, and the recently-built lodge that sits atop this river is just magnificent in its position.

The Nordura river is not very far from Reykjavik, the capital of Iceland, and runs through the Borgarfjordur region. It is not at all uncommon for this diverse river to produce over 2,000 salmon in a season. There are over 100 named pools within 34 miles on the Nordura, with the hours for fishing being from 7am to 1pm, and then again from 4pm through to 10pm. The number of anglers who can fish these rivers is of course tightly restricted, and the maximum allowed on the Nordura at any one time is fifteen. This is one of the rivers in Iceland that gives an angler a genuine chance at big salmon right at the start of June. Indeed, for most of the month large fish tend to enter the system. From the end of June there is then a strong run of grilse. Early season is a good time to use double-handed fly rods, due to the volume of water flowing through, but as levels drop then you can change over to a single-handed approach and smaller flies.

Best times to fish

There is good fishing nearly all year round, with summer being the best for numbers of fish. Winter, though, is the time for the biggest coalfish

Fishing methods

Lure and bait, with fly fishing close by for salmon and sea trout

Getting there

Saltstraumen is near to Bodo in northern Norway, just above the Arctic Circle. You can easily connect to Bodo from Oslo

Tips and tricks

Spinning might work well, but you seriously need to gear up for the big coalfish and use proper heavy duty rods and reels

SALTSTRAUMEN, NORWAY
Home to the most powerful maelstrom in the world, and the fish love it

It is virtually impossible to describe the flow and surge of water around Saltstraumen, for the power and speed as this seething maelstrom literally roars through a 160-yard wide gap at speeds of up to 20 knots is literally awe-inspiring to see. It is nature almost showing off. This is the most powerful maelstrom in the world, comprising huge whirlpools that can be over 30 feet in diameter and perhaps 15 feet deep. It is created by strong currents that tear through the channels connecting two big fjords. Within a six-hour tidal period there can be over a billion cubic feet of water pushing through this narrow gap, with the fastest flows taking place around spring tides on the full and new moons. But as much as Saltstraumen is incredible in its own right, there does also happen to be plenty of good fishing around here.

Potentially you will find no better place for catching big coalfish from the shore than around Saltstraumen. Indeed, the world record was taken from here at just over 50lbs. These coalfish are immensely powerful and feed well on a rich diet of smaller fish that abound in these nutrient-rich waters. It is possible to fish for and catch coalfish all year round, but the best time for the biggest ones is during the winter months when it can get very cold for fishing. Many methods work well for the big coalfish, including spinning with traditional spinners and also using heavy casting jigs, as well as livebaiting with one of the smaller coalfish, which can be easily caught. Around Saltstraumen you can also fish for cod, salmon, sea trout and haddock. Winter again is the time when big cod can show up very close to shore, but they can be caught throughout most of the year if you go specifically for them. Halibut are also caught from the boats fishing around here, although a few dedicated locals do take the odd one from the shore.

One of the world's most truly ugly fish is caught around Saltstraumen, but what the wolf fish lacks in the looks department it makes up for when it comes to its eating qualities. One of the ways to catch one of these hideous but sometimes large fish is to put big fish baits tight down on the bottom, literally right off the edge of the rocks, inside the main current. Use heavy enough weights to combat the depth and flow, and then make sure to sometimes bounce your weight up and down on the bottom to attract the wolf fish, which is known to be very inquisitive. Just make sure to keep away from those jaws if you manage to land one.

Best times to fish
The summer months, generally late April through to early September, with the early season being best for the halibut

Fishing methods
Lure, bait and even fly fishing

Getting there
There is a regular ferry service that takes people out to the islands. This runs from Bodo on the mainland, where you can also connect very easily from Oslo

Tips and tricks
Many anglers obsess with catching a big cod, but coalfish leave them for dead. Soft plastic shads or paddletails mounted on jig heads work really well for both species

LOFOTEN ISLANDS, NORWAY
World class saltwater fishing lying within the cold waters of the Arctic Circle

Some 60 miles off the port of Bodo, just above the Arctic Circle in Norway, lie the bottom two islands in the Lofoten chain, Rost and Vaeroy. These islands might be small in size, but the level of saltwater fishing they can offer gives a glimpse into how fish-rich so much of the coastline of Norway is. To fly anglers this wonderful country is known primarily as a big river, big salmon destination, but increasingly to saltwater anglers Norway is seen as arguably the best place to go and fish for big cod, coalfish and halibut. Coldwater fishing it might well be, but a big halibut can put so much heat on an angler that you can literally be brought to your knees as the fish dives. Big cod are huge fun, but perhaps the Lofoten Islands' best kept secret is the almost crazy numbers of large coalfish that swim these rich waters during the summer months. A coalfish is a true sporting species that will dive repeatedly.

Among the Lofoten Islands, it is Rost and Vaeroy that are most set up for sport fishing, with a few small fishing camps/lodges and various boats and skippers available to take clients out for the fishing. The best of the fishing is during the summer months when for a while there is virtually 24 hour daylight, enabling you to fish as much as your body can take.

Many other places, particularly in northern Norway, produce bigger cod than Rost and Vaeroy, but what sets these islands apart is that most of the fishing is done in relatively shallow water, which means you can use more sporting tackle and really get to enjoy the experience much more. There are still plenty of cod to over 40lbs in the Lofoten waters, but the unique draw to these remote islands is the halibut and coalfish fishing. The back-breaking experience of catching potentially huge halibut in shallow water is hard to describe, especially as halibut look like nothing more than giant flatfish. But despite appearances, they regularly break both rods and anglers' spirits. Halibut weighing just over 400lbs have been caught in these waters. Norway is awash with coalfish, particularly during the summer months and, believe it or not, a part of the problem in trying to find the bigger 20lb plus fish is that there are just too many small ones around that rob the lures and baits on the way down. Rost and Vaeroy do not tend to have these kinds of problems, however, and coalfish out here are regularly taken to over 30lbs, with fish of more than 40lbs caught every year.

Norwegian
Sea

Namsen river

Finland

Norway

Sweden

Best times to fish
Norway's salmon season
runs from 1 June to 31
August, although there
are often local variations

Fishing methods
Principally fly fishing

Getting there
Best airport access is
Trondheim, with plenty
of local and international
connections in and out

Tips and tricks
Prepare for almost any
weather, from baking hot
to torrential rain and cold

NAMSEN RIVER, NORWAY
'The Queen of Rivers' is a perfectly magical place to fish for salmon

Norway boasts a number of world class Atlantic salmon rivers, including the very
exclusive and hideously expensive Alta in the north, where every year some huge salmon
are caught. But this country also has some far more accessible rivers like the Namsen, which
offers over 100 miles of salmon fishing. This magical river throws up some huge fish from time
to time too; in 2006, for example, there was a salmon of just over 50lbs caught here. The
largest recorded rod-caught salmon on the Namsen weighed 69lbs, caught in 1924. The mind
somewhat boggles at an Atlantic salmon this big. However, you will also find very strong runs of
medium-sized fish and grilse.

Much of the salmon fishing on the Namsen river takes place on the stretch of river known as
the Upper Namsen, principally around the small town of Grong, which is of course very geared up
for visiting anglers. There is plenty of accommodation that is close to the river to take advantage
of the long daylight hours during mid-summer. The Namsen itself starts in the Børgefjell National

Park and runs for nearly 125 miles until it empties into its estuary near the town of Namsos. The upper part of the river is equipped with eight hydro–electric dams, which actually have the distinct advantage of providing some regular and stable water conditions for salmon fishing. It was the British who first stumbled upon the fishing potential in the Namsen and they named it 'The Queen of Rivers'. It was not long until plenty of keen British salmon anglers were making the trek for the high numbers of large fish.

The famous Fiskum Falls beat offers almost a mile of bank fishing on both sides, and with the addition of a large salmon ladder, the fish can now swim above these 37-yard falls. But what was once a natural barrier is still a very good holding pool for the fish before some of them try to negotiate the ladder.

The Ovre Media and Fossland beats make up the rest of the Upper Namsen, and there are 13 named pools that are full of variety and interest. 'Harling' is one of the most traditional ways to fish the Namsen, where the fly angler fishes from a boat with a rower, but around the Upper Namsen especially, there are plenty of places to fish successfully from the banks. The best time to fish for big salmon is usually in June, with 20 June to 20 July offering the most prolific runs of fish. However, do not for one second discount the fishing into August when there is every chance of hooking a grilse or a very large cock salmon on the same swing through.

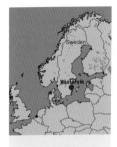

Best times to fish
Generally late June into
September. Ice fishing
for pike does take place
during the winter, but
that tends to be on the
inland freshwater lakes,
of which there are plenty

Fishing methods
Lure, fly and bait

Getting there
Västervik is easily
accessed from Stockholm

Tips and tricks
There is not much that
Swedish pike anglers
don't know about lure
fishing. Watch and learn

VÄSTERVIK, SWEDEN
Pike and Sweden go together like GTs and the Seychelles

Unless you have been to Sweden, it is hard to understand just how big pike fishing is in this wonderful country. As US freshwater anglers might fish for largemouth bass, so Swedish anglers will fish for pike. Sweden has so much pike fishing water that in some respects it is impossible to know where to begin. There are over 100,000 inland freshwater lakes for starters. The Västervik archipelago, which lies in the south-east of the country on the Baltic coastline, is an area well worth considering for pike as well as for zander, ide, bream, roach, rudd and then, out at sea, cod and salmon (there are plenty of smaller fish for the predatory pike to feed on). Trolling for big Baltic salmon is another very popular way to fish around here, especially during the cold winter months. The zander tend to favour much deeper and colder water.

Västervik is somewhat unique in that many of these lakes on the Baltic coastline are actually brackish water because they connect to the sea. It is hard to comprehend the extent to which pike fishing is a national obsession in Sweden, and when the weather and conditions are favourable you will see plenty of anglers out fishing. If you fish with a good local guide though, you can easily escape the crowds and find yourself in perfect seclusion. Take a look at a map of Sweden to try and get your head around just how much water there is here to fish.

Spring is perhaps the best time to try and catch the biggest pike, and ones weighing over 40lbs have been caught in the Västervik area. Anglers will generally look to fish the rather deeper areas in spring where the big female pike will be hanging around waiting for the correct conditions to spawn. As the water then begins to warm up into summer, so the fishing tends to switch over to the many underwater islands lying in shallower water as well as the multitude of shallow bays and inlets. The best time to fish these particular areas is when the wind direction helps to drive in the baitfish. It is worth noting that the vast majority of pike fishing in Sweden takes place from a boat, and lure fishing is by far the most popular way to catch them. However, do not discount bait or fly fishing, although undoubtedly a boat and lure fishing tackle do give you the ability to effectively cover large amounts of water when on the hunt for pike.

North
Sea

Lough Mask
Lough Corrib

Ireland

United
Kingdom

Best times to fish
It is a long season,
but generally April to
September would be
considered the best
times for trout fishing

Fishing methods
Fly fishing

Getting there
Each year it seems that
the road network in
Ireland is getting better
and better, and the wild
west coast is far more
easily accessible these
days from major airports
like Dublin

Tips and tricks
Weather on these
loughs is key, both for
the actual fishing and
as to whether you can
safely fish from a boat

LOUGH MASK AND LOUGH CORRIB, IRELAND
Wild, rugged and full of truly wild brown trout

The rugged west coast of Ireland is beset with a number of big limestone loughs (lakes)
that tend to be incredibly clear, and these rich cold waters hold very healthy populations of wild
brown trout. Truly wild trout are unimaginably beautiful creatures, and the famous Lough Mask
and Lough Corrib are but two of the most well-known waterways to go and fish for them (Lough
Mask empties into the Corrib River, which in turn runs into Lough Corrib. These two loughs are
therefore very much connected to each other). The chance to catch a wild brown that might
well weigh over 5lbs is a serious draw, and some hardcore anglers even go trolling the deeper
water for the huge ferox trout (cannibal browns) that can reach over 20lbs in Corrib. What might
surprise some people is that the fishing is free, and the season runs from 15 February to
30 September. Turn up and go trout fishing, although it would be wise to hire a good local guide
to help you cope with such large waters. In Ireland this guide or boatman is known as a ghillie.

Lough Mask is over 20,000 acres in size, and it sits where the central limestone plains come together with the sandstone mountains of the beautiful Mayo region. Scotland might well have some of the most famous salmon rivers in the world, but the west coast of Ireland is without doubt one of the most special areas on earth. The clear waters of somewhere like Lough Mask produce very good numbers of wild browns that might average over the 1lb mark; indeed 2-3lb fish are more than common. Mask is huge, and the use of a professional guide is a very sensible way to maximise your time and get to grips with just so much water and so many fish-holding features. The sheer scale of shallow bays, rocky shorelines, islands and river mouths is enough to give any visiting angler second thoughts about where to fish, especially when considering that it is in fact the deeper water that most consistently produces trout on dry flies.

Perhaps the most traditionally popular and arguably most efficient way to fish for wild browns on these huge waterways is to do so from a boat with relatively long fly rods and floating or slow sinking lines. Teams of wet flies are effective when there is cloud cover and the waves can help move the flies, but in more settled conditions the trout will perhaps take dry flies off the top. The start of the season is generally a time for the faster sinking lines to get down to the trout, but as early as late March and into April will see increased insect life and fish movements near the surface.

Best times to fish
You can fish the Shannon throughout the year, but spring through to autumn tends to be best

Fishing methods
Lure, bait and fly

Getting there
Kilrush is a good place to access the northern side of the estuary

Tips and tricks
Fresh mackerel tends to be the killer bait for bottom fishing in the Shannon

SHANNON ESTUARY, IRELAND

Tuck in here when the weather turns wild, for the west coast of Ireland is more than capable of throwing all four seasons at you in just one day

As much as the wild west coast of Clare in Ireland is a truly magical place to go fishing, this is the west coast, and the weather can do virtually anything within a day. However, never for a second let a bit of bad weather dampen your spirits, for close by is the mighty Shannon estuary, which can provide sheltered waters stashed full of fish. On a coastline as exposed as the west coast, it is indeed helpful to have such a huge sheltered waterway for those times when it's needed, although the Shannon is well worth exploring, whatever the weather.

The River Shannon starts in the mountains of West Cavan and runs roughly south for around 160 miles until it becomes tidal at Limerick. Saltwater fishing aside, the River Shannon and its many tributaries offer all manner of freshwater fishing for brown trout, salmon and various other non-game species such as pike and bream. The best game fishing tends to be found within the

tributaries off the main river, and also in the three large loughs of Allen, Ree and Derg.

It can actually be somewhat disconcerting to be able to head so far inland from the coastline and still catch saltwater species. You can be fishing from the banks of the estuary over 30 miles from the sea and yet be catching thornback rays, bass and bull huss; indeed the murky waters of the Shannon at times seem like they are literally full of rays and huss. There is generally no need to fish at night because all the principal species are as prevalent here during daylight hours. If you bottom fish with mackerel and squid baits, you will always be in with a chance of catching 10lb plus rays and huss. At times small to medium-sized tope will also run up the estuary and give you a rather explosive bite.

The Shannon estuary has become increasingly famous for being home to Ireland's only resident group of bottlenose dolphins, and you can book a trip out to see them from places such as Kilrush. There are also a number of professional charter fishing boats that take anglers out into the Shannon and then, weather permitting, further on out into the Atlantic. The harbours, marinas and quiet creeks are good places to go looking for shoals of grey mullet, but as is always the case with these shy fish, a concerted effort at keeping quiet and low down always pays dividends.

Best times to fish
There can be good fishing year round, but look to concentrate your efforts from about May to the end of October. There can be some good winter bass fishing on the beaches when conditions are right

Fishing methods
Lure, bait and fly

Getting there
Readily accessible from Dublin and Cork, County Clare is easy to get around

Tips and tricks
Many of the locals for some reason are convinced that mullet are impossible to catch, but use good groundbait and either mackerel flesh or sliced white bread for bait and they will feed

CLARE COASTLINE, IRELAND
Achingly beautiful, very underfished and full of untapped potential

The rugged west coast of Ireland in County Clare is all about rock and beach fishing, but this is one part of the world in which to take serious care when it comes to the sea conditions. Catch it right and it's like fishing on some kind of parallel earth that nobody has yet discovered, but when the weather turns you need to get off the rocks and seek shelter either inside the huge Shannon estuary or otherwise in a local pub.

A good area to base yourself to access the different kinds of fishing is the small town of Kilkee, to the south of which is the imposing Loop Head. Around here, wherever you can find safe and easy access to the water's edge you will literally be able to catch some fish. Use spinning gear off the rocks for pollack and plenty of mackerel in summer, and then drop crab and worm baits close in for hordes of ravenous wrasse. Within the entrance to the bay at Kilkee are rocks that uncover at low water; if the conditions are too rough outside the bay, then just drop back in here and spin for pollack along the edges. You can also groundbait for some big mullet here, but don't be surprised if some aggressive triggerfish soon turn up and start attacking your mullet float. These fish can be caught on more regular baits.

If you want to catch conger eels then head out onto the rocks at night, but unless you are used to this kind of shore fishing, it might be wiser to make your way instead to one of the many local pubs and get a taste of the 'craic' that Ireland is so rightly famous for. There is always tomorrow for the fishing after all, and if the pub has some live entertainment then you could be in for a fun night.

A number of classic surf beaches along the Clare coastline will all throw up good bass fishing when the conditions are moderately onshore and kicking up a bit of a surf. Bass respond well to these conditions, and for the most part you want to consider bottom fishing baits such as peeler crab, lugworm and sandeels. Look for areas of shallow, rocky and broken ground to go and fish lures for bass. Note that spring tides tend to work better for this style of fishing, but good conditions are vital. Mullet can be found around Kilkee and also at the few small harbours to the south of the town on the inside of the peninsula.

Best times to fish
There is good shore fishing year round, but the best time for pollack is generally around May through to October. Evenings are always good times for Irish pollack

Fishing methods
Lure, bait and fly

Getting there
A fairly easy drive from the ferries that come into Rosslare, or fly into Cork airport and pick up a hire car

Tips and tricks
Pollack will sometimes respond to different colour lures, so make sure you keep on swapping until you hit fish. They often like dark colours

THE BEARA PENINSULA, IRELAND
There is every chance you can find spots literally never fished by anybody before

For such a relatively small country, Ireland has one of the most exciting and dramatic coastlines for fishing anywhere in Europe. If you get off the beaten track and explore a little, it is very unlikely that you will ever see another angler out on the rugged and remote Beara peninsula. The Ring of Kerry to the north quite rightly grabs a large share of fishing interest, but the quiet and staggeringly beautiful Beara is like a shore fishing heaven all by itself. Whatever the weather is doing or however hard the wind is blowing, there will always be somewhere to tuck away from it and carry on fishing. Up in those misty hills there is also a network of wild loughs that more often than not have perfect wild brown trout in them and cost nothing to fish. Ireland has literally everything that an angler could possibly want, but the west coast is not as green as it is for no good reason. Carry waterproofs at all times, as the weather can change so quickly here.

The Beara is principally about rock fishing for fish such as pollack, conger eels, wrasse, bull huss and different ray species like the thornback and small-eyed. Pollack fishing with light

spinning gear somewhere around the Dursey Island area tends to feel like fishing at the edge of the world; indeed, the next stop to the west of here is the USA. Take huge care in rough conditions though, for the swells that pound these rugged shores at times can be extremely dangerous if you get too close to the water's edge. If it's too rough, then just consult a map and go and find some shelter – with all those headlands and bays, this is never very difficult to do. If you get it right with regards to the pollack, then these gloriously unsubtle, crash-diving fish will wrench your arms off for hours on end, and in general the flooding tide is when they feed the hardest.

Big shoals of mullet can and do turn up almost anywhere around the Beara, and if you want to really target them then make sure to groundbait around sheltered bays and harbours like Castletownbere. When mullet come on the feed in Ireland they can sometimes go a bit crazy, although of course there are also plenty of times when these conniving fish can drive any angler to the edge of madness with their sheer tenacity. If you do manage to hook one on light freshwater fishing tackle, you will see what all the fuss is about as it runs and runs. The Beara is not known for bass fishing, but if you take a look around you will see plenty of appealing locations if you want to have a go. Although bass are caught here, it tends to be kept fairly quiet.

Best times to fish
Generally from around
May into October, but
the weather can and
will do everything at
any time of the year

Fishing methods
Lure, bait and fly.
Fly fishing for pollack
is huge fun

Getting there
The islands all have
various ferry services
from different places
up and down the west
coast. Most are very
easily accessible

Tips and tricks
Pollack often respond
best to darker coloured
lures and the best fish
tend to hug the bottom

WEST COAST ISLANDS, IRELAND
Most people have no idea how far from the beaten track you can get in Ireland

Much of the western coastline of Ireland is rugged enough already, and in truth the potential for shore fishing is just vast. But it is perfectly possible to get even further away from the already distinct lack of anglers and head for one of the remote islands that almost litter the west coast. Islands such as Inishbofin, Inishturk, Inishark, Clare, Achill and the larger Aran islands off the coast of Galway are surrounded by the cold, fish-rich waters of the Atlantic Ocean, and recreational fishing pressure is essentially zero. There is no angling infrastructure to speak of and you are always going to be gambling with the weather in this part of the world. However, the simple fact that you can catch ferries to these islands and simply walk, hike, scramble and fish until you drop, as well as most likely see no other angler all day or indeed all week, is what makes all the extra effort worthwhile. Ireland is a sport fishing gem, and as much as it tends to be the game and freshwater fishing that is perhaps best known about, many anglers would argue that it is Ireland's mostly deserted coastline that offers the greatest rewards. This is some truly wild fishing.

Without doubt the principal quarry when you go fishing around any of these islands is going to be the pollack. Ireland is awash with good pollack fishing, and there are still many locations that have most likely never been seen by an angler. The trick to finding pollack in Ireland is to look for rocks, rocks and more rocks. If you are happy to clamber over rocks and look for water with a bit of depth close to shore then you are certainly in with a chance. Pollack will always be found around structure, whether that be rocks, reefs, pinnacles or drop-offs. Pollack fishing perfectly suits the angler who is interested in visiting these remote islands and travelling light, for you can easily get away with a simple spinning rod and reel plus various hard and soft lures. They are a gloriously unsubtle kind of fish in that they will always try and crash-dive for the bottom when hooked. Pollack usually feed hardest in Ireland just as dusk gives way to darkness.

Anywhere you find rock and weed will also most likely be crawling with the hard-fighting wrasse, and at night over the same kind of ground you can often catch conger eels and maybe some bull huss. The whole crux of this Irish island hopping is that the anglers have to make it up as they go along and use their saltwater skills to help them discover the whereabouts of the fish. But this is Ireland, and these waters contain an abundance of fish. Catching a few fresh mackerel and barbecuing them as you fish with the Atlantic Ocean stretching out in front of you is about as good as life is ever going to get.

Best times to fish
Saltwater fishing is possible all year round, especially bass in winter on bait. Salmon and sea trout are best from 17 January to 30 September, and brown trout from 15 February to 30 September

Fishing methods
Bait, lure and fly

Getting there
Places such as Waterville, Tralee and Ballybunion give good access to lots of fishing in Kerry. Drive there from the Rosslare ferry or fly into Shannon, Kerry and Cork airports

Tips and tricks
Onshore conditions for bass fishing are always the best

KERRY, IRELAND
All four seasons a possibility in every single perfect day on Ireland's rugged south-west coast

The staggeringly beautiful county Kerry region on the south-west coast of Ireland is home to some of the finest and most unspoilt fishing in northern Europe, with all manner of saltwater and freshwater species available for all kinds of anglers.

The extensive and mainly rugged coastline is perfect for bass fishing with bait and lures. Although these majestic fish can be caught all year round, it is often the colder months when you find the most consistent fishing for the larger bass, which are taken from the beaches and rocks on bottom-fished baits. For some reason bass fishing in Ireland is arguably more successful during daylight hours, whereas in the UK, for example, you would expect to catch more at night.

As is the case throughout much of Ireland, Kerry is beset with plenty of mullet, yet strangely so few local anglers ever think to fish for them. Sometimes referred to as 'Europe's answer to the bonefish', grey mullet offer a wonderful challenge in saltwater for anglers prepared to scale down and use lighter freshwater tactics or even try fly fishing for them. Large shoals of mullet can often

be enticed close to shore and almost 'held' there via the use of various fish-based groundbaits.

Kerry provides a large variety of more general saltwater fishing from the rocks and beaches, including some outstanding sport for the often very obliging pollack. Without doubt the best time to look for pollack in Ireland is around last light as they rise up higher in the water column to feed eagerly before night sets in. Regular spinning tactics with soft and hard lures can work well, but make sure you play these fish hard as they are very prone to crash-diving straight for a rocky sanctuary when hooked. Take the road bridge over to Valentia Island and spend time on the western side fishing some very deep water for species such as conger eels, bull huss, mackerel and even codling at range during the summer months. Real care must be taken when fishing these waters either in rough onshore conditions or when there is a big Atlantic swell rolling in.

The freshwater fly fisherman is also well looked after in Kerry, but it would be a shame not to use the fly gear on the salt as well. Not far from the coast, at Waterville, lies the large and very famous Lough Currane. Here you will find plenty of boats and local guides available to take you out and try for the early spring salmon and sea trout running up from the 200-yard stretch of Butler's Pool and into the lough. There are a number of smaller, wild rivers and loughs up in the hills that are often full of perfectly formed wild brown trout, and sometimes these more inaccessible waterways are entirely free to fish.

Best times to fish
Generally May to November. Sharks turn up around the middle of June and stay into October if conditions are favourable

Fishing methods
Mostly bait and lure, but there is plenty of wild freshwater fly fishing around if you go looking for it

Getting there
Baltimore is about a two-hour drive west of Cork

Tips and tricks
The big fish might be the main attraction, but well over 40 species of fish have been caught from these waters. Enjoy the variety on offer

BALTIMORE, IRELAND
Hook a skate bigger than a barn door and your back might never forgive you

The village of Baltimore in West Cork might not be as famous as Dingle or Kinsale, but this sleepy place is one of Ireland's saltwater fishing hotspots, with some seriously good boat fishing and endless shore fishing opportunities. If you want to try and catch a huge common skate then this is without doubt one of the best places to try, although somewhere like Oban on the west coast of Scotland is also worth bearing in mind. Common skate are not in fact common, as their name might suggest, but these days you can experience some good fishing for them if you fish with the right people in the right places. Like anywhere that is exposed to the wild Atlantic Ocean, fishing around Baltimore is very much dependent on the weather but, if needs be, there is usually somewhere your skipper can tuck away and fish.

The wild south-west coastline of Ireland juts out into the warmer, plankton-rich waters of the Gulf Stream, and this promotes all kinds of fish to come close inshore. In the summer months the local charter boats can catch good numbers of the sleek and stunning blue sharks without having to steam far from land at all. Most commonly the boats will drift the best areas and floatfish fish baits for these ocean-wandering predators. Closer in again, over all the rocky pinnacles, there is always the chance to hook up with a porbeagle shark. These fish are different to blue sharks in that they will come very close inshore and use the rocks and reefs as cover to hunt for prey species like pollack. Over this rough ground you can spend a great deal of time just having huge amounts of fun fishing for pollack, ling, cod, coalfish and conger eels, and not far from the rugged coastline lie many wrecks over which you can catch these species too. Bluefin and albacore tuna have been caught here as well.

Baltimore, however, is one of the recognised places to try and catch a big common skate. Although not electric fighters, these big rays are still going to pull seriously hard and test you to the limit. The fact that you pull these fish up from deep water is a part of what makes fishing for them so unique; indeed they are not running away from you as a tarpon or a shark might be. Big skate do not like coming up off the bottom and that desire to remain there translates to the angler, who is holding a buckled, straining fishing rod. Skate over 200lbs have been taken from Baltimore waters, and plenty are caught over the 100lb mark. When it comes to saltwater fishing, the south-west of Ireland is undoubtedly an incredibly special place, boasting some seriously fish-rich waters.

Best times to fish
Around end of April to the end of October. There is a bass fishing close season in Ireland from 15 May to 15 June

Fishing methods
Lure, bait and fly

Getting there
A relatively easily accessible coastline with plenty of roads and paths, but the best fishing is often off the beaten track

Tips and tricks
Make sure to carry waterproofs at all times. You can get four seasons in one day in Ireland

COPPER COAST, IRELAND
One of Europe's finest stretches of bass fishing coastlines

It is hard to think of a more perfect stretch of coastline in northern Europe for going bass fishing than the Copper Coast in southern Ireland. Take all the ideal terrains and habitats for bass, drop them into a comparatively small area, and then leave the place alone to the mercy of the wind and waves to forever tempt anglers who are prepared to get off the beaten track and explore as part of their fishing. If you take a look at the coastline from Dungarven to Tramore, this section of southern Ireland is about as good as bass fishing is going to get, and there are any number of out of the way locations where you can fish by yourself all day and night long.

The extensive bay and estuary system around the town of Dungarven is a good place to start, for it is a well kept secret in bass fishing circles. When the fishing is on, the sheer numbers of bass caught from these often very sheltered waters can sometimes almost defy belief. From around mid-March through to as late as the end of December, the larger spring tides can produce bass on bait and lures, but prime times would be the end of April through to the end of October.

There are also huge numbers of mullet milling around all over the place, especially in the tidal pools created by the various rivers and streams clearing into the bay. Make sure to check them out for bass as well.

The Copper Coast is the stretch of coastline roughly from Dungarven east to Tramore, and for around 25 miles it offers all manner of hidden coves, beaches and treacherous boulder fields that are perfect bass habitats. There is no easy way to go about fishing this rugged coastline other than to go looking for places you can get access to, but be very careful not to get cut off by a big rising tide. It is always tempting to try and find what might be just around the corner, so make sure you always know the times of high and low tide.

The whole Copper Coast essentially faces due south, so as much as gentle to moderate winds from the south to south-west are ideal for bass fishing here, the generally shallow ground can quickly become too rough and coloured for lure fishing if the winds are too strong. But there is always the backup of the large Dungarven bay, or otherwise tuck away a bit and fish on the bottom with bait for the bass. You can also fish for pollack and wrasse at any number of spots along this wonderful stretch of coastline, and at Tramore there is a huge surf beach that fishes well at night when there is some sea running from an onshore wind.

Best times to fish
Can fish all year round for many species, but best for bass from May to end of October

Fishing methods
Lure, fly and bait

Getting there
Easily accessed from the various ferries that come into Rosslare, plus Dublin, Waterford and even Cork airports are not far away at all

Tips and tricks
Many of the rock locations fish well for bass as the tide is going out (ebbing)

SOUTH-EAST COASTLINE, IRELAND
A hidden saltwater fishing paradise tucked away in a quiet corner of Ireland

One of Ireland's hidden gems, the south-east corner of the Emerald Isle offers some of the country's finest and most consistent saltwater fishing for any number of species, including bass, tope, smoothhounds, rays, flounders, mullet, pollack and wrasse. Beset with a magical mix of rocks, estuaries, open beaches and harbours, the south-east coastline has the lot, yet so many anglers drive straight on by in their quest to see and fish the admittedly wonderful and utterly stunning west and south-west coasts.

When it comes to shore fishing for bass, there are arguably no finer areas than those found around this rugged but easily accessible coastline. A great place to base yourself to take advantage of some world class bass fishing would be somewhere like Fethard-on-Sea, which sits close to the banks of the fascinating Bannow estuary. The area immediately surrounding the famous town of Wexford is equally worth a visit. What this coastline does offer the more adventurous bass angler is some kind of shelter, whichever way the wind blows or whatever the conditions are like. If the generally south facing coastline is blown out for bass fishing, you can

usually find a headland to tuck behind or otherwise seek shelter within an estuary such as the Bannow. It is often the case in Ireland that the largest bass are taken from sheltered estuaries.

Around the south-eastern tip of Ireland at Rosslare and the numerous surrounding beaches, you can come across some very good shore fishing for fast-running fish such as smoothhounds and tope. The tides around Rosslare can be particularly ferocious, but then this is what draws in so many fish. Always take great care when wading out for any kind of shore fishing.

One of Ireland's most untalked about fisheries is for mullet, an often overlooked species that is almost ridiculously abundant in so many parts of the country. The famous Kilmore Quay is a good place to start looking for these often hard to catch fish, but mullet are always worth spending a bit of time on. Make sure you check out the various estuaries as well as open coast locations where the mullet can be groundbaited in at times. Professional charter fishing boats run out of Kilmore Quay, and this whole south-eastern corner has always been a very popular area for anglers who like to bring their own boats.

The winter cod fishing in the extensive Waterford estuary seems to be getting better and better each year, with crab and lugworm being the best baits. There are plenty of spots that offer easy access to deeper water very close to shore, and don't forget that this estuary system is full of hungry flounders as well as some big bass at times.

Best times to fish
Spring and summer
are usually the best
times for salmon fishing,
with fresh spring fish
in particular being
something very special

Fishing methods
Predominantly fly fishing,
but some lure and bait
fishing is permitted.
This very much depends
upon each particular
beat though

Getting there
Easily accessible by road
or from Inverness and
Aberdeen airports

Tips and tricks
Traditionally the third
week of June is when
the runs of grilse
start to appear

RIVER SPEY, SCOTLAND
One of the homes of Atlantic salmon fishing

There can be little doubt that the River Spey is just about the most famous Atlantic salmon fishing river in the world; indeed it is also where Spey casting originally comes from. This mighty river rises in the Monadhliath mountains, which lie south of Loch Ness, and then it flows for roughly 100 miles in a northerly direction until it empties into the Moray Firth at Spey Bay. The water downstream from Grantown gives anglers miles and miles of fly fishing for salmon, sea trout and trout. It is worth noting that the upper reaches can be excellent for the trout fishing, if not for salmon. The salmon fishing, however, is why the Spey is so famous worldwide. Tributaries of the Spey such as the River Avon and the River Dulnain are in their own rights also pretty serious salmon rivers. The River Avon flows out of Loch Avon in the Cairngorm mountains and winds for 40 miles before joining the Spey at Ballindalloch. From April onwards its clear waters tend to have a good run of salmon and sea trout. In fishing terms the Spey can be divided up into the Upper Spey (from source to Boat of Garten), Middle Spey (Grantown to Aberlour) and Lower Spey (Aberlour to Spey Bay).

Anybody who knows something about the history of Atlantic salmon fishing will have heard of famous beats on the Spey, with names such as Tulchan, Castle Grant, Rothes, Arndilly, Delfur and Carron. However, many of these stretches of water are, of course, tightly controlled. But as much as numerous beats are almost jealously guarded through the prime times of April, May, June and July (for example, Arndilly in May or Tulchan in July), thankfully there are various angling associations which control some very good stretches of river and make them readily available to visiting anglers. Known as Association Water, it's another reason why the Spey is so special, in that anglers who do not have access to the often very expensive private waters can still experience some historic salmon fishing for sensible money.

Although the River Spey is renowned for its salmon fishing, it is perhaps also the finest sea trout river in Scotland. For the most part the best sea trout fishing happens above Grantown, but this is partly down to the fact that lower down the river the majority of anglers are, of course, fixated upon catching salmon. The fish still have to swim past them on their way upriver. There is also some outstanding wild brown trout fishing along the Spey, and permits are generally very much available throughout the less well-known upper reaches of the river via the Badenoch Angling Association.

Best times to fish
The trout season starts around 1 April and then runs generally until the end of September. Some rivers allow winter grayling fishing

Fishing methods
Fly only, and generally upstream dry fly fishing unless a particular river allows upstream nymph fishing after a certain date

Getting there
Very easy access to all the rivers

Tips and tricks
Late afternoons and early evening often see most trout rising

SOUTHERN CHALKSTREAMS, ENGLAND
About as gloriously and quintessentially English as fly fishing can get

Arguably the birthplace of fly fishing as we know it today, the world famous, clear running chalkstreams of southern England offer some classical fly fishing for brown trout especially, but also for salmon, sea trout, pike and chub on certain stretches of some of the rivers.

The Test, the Kennet and the Itchen are perhaps the most famous of the southern chalkstreams and, as such, they can command some very high prices to fish some of the most revered and talked-about beats. It is even the case that some private beats are open only to various club members and their guests, but there are also plenty of rivers or specific stretches of river that offer comparable fly fishing for a fraction of the price, and it is still possible to find some wonderful fly fishing for the generally smaller but very feisty wild brown trout. Other rivers include the Anton, Avon, Dever, Nadder, Wylye and the Ebble. Every chalkstream has its own unique charms, with some being so well prepared and looked after that they could almost be called

manicured, whereas others offer a somewhat different and perhaps more 'wild' experience.

For the most part, these chalkstreams are all about upstream dry fly fishing for brown trout, but on a few of them you are allowed to fish using upstream nymph tactics at certain times of the year. You can also access some often cheap and quite wonderful winter grayling fishing on a number of chalkstreams, and on a cold, crisp morning this can be fantastic sport. The grayling fishing takes place from October through to early March.

One of the most famous aspects to this chalkstream fly fishing is the annual mayfly hatch, which is sometimes referred to as 'Duffers' Fortnight' because of the trout's increased feeding frenzy on these large hatching flies. In theory, this hatch of mayflies is roughly a two-week period when the trout tend to go on a binge, although many factors contribute towards when these flies hatch out each season. Traditionally the prime time might well have been May, but it is often the case that the best fishing comes around early June, with late afternoons and early evenings being the best times to see big numbers of trout rising. The mayfly hatch is often the time when the largest wild brown trout are taken, and it needs to be noted that many of the chalkstreams are also fished more heavily during this period. Little, though, is as exciting as watching a big trout rise up in crystal clear water to take a fly off the surface, and even better if that fly is attached to your leader.

North
Sea

Ireland

United
Kingdom

Chesil Beach

Best times to fish
All year round for
numerous species,
but September to
usually about the end
of January for the cod

Fishing methods
Bait and lure

Getting there
Chesil Beach is in Dorset.
The closest large town
is Weymouth, to the
east of the beach

Tips and tricks
Good quality bait will
always pay dividends

CHESIL BEACH, ENGLAND

Somewhat daunting if you don't know where to fish, but a beach that can throw up almost any species of UK saltwater fish

Even on its own, the mighty Chesil Beach is a site to behold. Around 17 miles long, it forms part of the renowned Jurassic Coast, which is England's only natural World Heritage Site. Chesil Beach is also a shore fishing mecca for any number of species throughout the year. It is a unique beach of sorts in that it tends to slope very steeply and, as such, offers easy access to deep water close in. A few small areas of the beach are out of bounds due to being part of the nature reserve, but in general this vast expanse of shingle can be fished almost from the Isle of Portland at its eastern end right along to Bridport at its western extremity.

Almost every fishable species that swims in UK waters has been caught from Chesil Beach at some time or another, and although to the untrained eye it might look like a somewhat featureless expanse of shingle, the fishing itself varies greatly along its length. Chesil has for years been rightly famous for its early autumn and early winter cod fishing, and in general the fishing really gets going sometime in September, depending on conditions. September to November are prime times, with most big fish showing either during moderate onshore conditions (southerly and south-westerly winds), or otherwise immediately after a really big blow. Whiting tend to turn up in real numbers from around November.

Plenty of flatfish, including plaice and sole, are caught from the beach, with locations such as West Bexington and Cogden being fairly consistent. However, you need to be aware of the annual invasion of spider crabs from around May into summer, which makes bait fishing on the bottom difficult at times. A wealth of mackerel can be caught all along the beach on warm summer days, but occasionally the popular spots get very crowded with anglers. The wreck of the Royal Adelaide lies about 100 yards offshore and can produce all manner of different species, including triggerfish and black bream in summer and early autumn. Access this spot from the Chesil Beach Centre car park just beyond Ferrybridge.

One little known fact about Chesil Beach is that it does throw up good numbers of bass to a few dedicated lure anglers who really know the ins and outs of the different locations and conditions required. Just turning up and expecting to catch fish is not the way to tackle a place like Chesil, so do all you can to source some up-to-date local knowledge from the tackle shops in Weymouth, for example. Some of the best bass fishing can be towards the Portland end of the beach, but always make sure you keep your eyes open for signs of smaller baitfish being hit from beneath or birds working.

Best times to fish
Generally summer
and autumn

Fishing methods
Bait for the barbel,
but they do take flies
sometimes. Fly fishing for
trout and salmon

Getting there
The River Wye for much
of its course runs along
the border between
England and Wales.
Easily accessible

Tips and tricks
Take the more classical
approach to the barbel
fishing and really give in
to this gloriously British
way of freshwater fishing

RIVER WYE, UK
Blessed are the rivers in which the magnificent barbel swim

The River Wye runs for over 150 miles from the slopes of the Welsh mountains at Plynlimon
to the River Severn, which then drains into the murky and extremely tidal Bristol Channel. There
is plenty of good fishing all along the picturesque River Wye, but without a doubt it is the mighty
barbel that sits at the top of any freshwater angler's list. Fish the right stretches with the right
people and barbel fishing in the Wye is how fishing is meant to be. Wild fish, very few people and
stunning surroundings. Much of the Lower Wye Valley is an Area of Outstanding Natural Beauty.

There are two principal ways to fish for barbel. Either you fish in a light, mobile and arguably
more natural way, or else you can take a 'carp fishing' type of approach and spend a lot of time in
specific areas with plenty of bait in the water to entice the fish. There are stretches of the Wye in
Hereford, especially, that are wonderfully conducive to fishing for barbel the proper way; indeed if
the river conditions are right you can on occasion sight fish to them in the clear water. Carp-style

tactics might over time produce the absolute largest fish, but sometimes it is the overall experience that can bring about more pleasure.

The River Wye is at its most picturesque during summer and autumn, and these glorious times of the year are when the barbel fishing is generally at its finest, although if you get good conditions then it is perfectly possible to catch big barbel in winter too. What tends to ruin it more than anything is an abundance of extra water in the river after heavy rains. The Wye has for many years been famous for salmon fishing, producing some huge Atlantic salmon, but the numbers of fish have sadly dwindled over the years. However, perhaps with the measures being taken to try and restore the fishing, it might well claw its way back and rival some of the famous Scottish rivers.

The Wye is primarily a game fishing river for trout, salmon and grayling above the town of Hay-on-Wye, but there are some good chub and pike if you go looking for them. The upper reaches of the river offer some truly wild and personal fly fishing, but it is the middle reaches which might be described as providing a classic kind of freshwater (coarse) fishing. The middle and lower reaches are where the barbel fishing takes place, and the famous Wye and Usk foundation runs three very good stretches below Hereford – White House, Caradoc and Backney. Day tickets are available.

Best times to fish
The salmon season is 1 February until 31 October, but the best times are May through to October. The brown and sea trout season starts on 15 March and ends 30 September

Fishing methods
Mainly fly fishing for the trout, salmon and sea trout, but after 16 June some anglers will fish with spinners and worms for the salmon

Getting there
Lynmouth is right on the edge of Exmoor National Park in North Devon. The closest large town is Barnstaple

Tips and tricks
Travel light and cover as much of this fabulous ground as you can

RIVER LYN, ENGLAND
Some delightfully subtle and accessible wild trout fishing set amongst a truly savage terrain

When it comes to fly fishing for trout, then England is perhaps most famous for its prolific and unique chalkstreams of Hampshire, Wiltshire and Dorset. The River Lyn in north Devon could not be more different to these rather gentle trout rivers. Indeed, any fly angler, when looking at the lower stretches of the Lyn as it tumbles into the old fishing harbour of Lynmouth on the edge of the wild and stunning Exmoor, could have a fright at the thought of actually fishing this little river. There are parts where certainly being a mountain goat might be useful, but taking a walk or a scramble down into the various gorges is like entering another quite wonderful world of fly fishing, where lawns are not mowed and riverbanks are not perfectly cut. You could argue that this is fly fishing for wild trout as it is meant to be.

The Lyn is a small spate river that is full of perfectly formed wild brown trout, but in times of rain or high spring tides then a number of salmon and sometimes sea trout will also start heading up the river. Salmon, especially, will begin to move up the river in late spring, but the numbers of fish are generally low. The more productive summer salmon run tends to start sometime in June when the water conditions are correct, and fish will keep moving in right into autumn. A lot of local salmon fishing on the Lyn is done with spinners and worms after 16 June.

Some stretches of the River Lyn require that the angler be on the fit side; indeed it is like stumbling upon a secret west country utopia as you walk down steep paths and then walk and wade entire sections made up of huge boulders, rocks, deep-sided valleys and trees everywhere. To be able to skilfully cast small flies on light fly rods is a huge advantage, especially if you can precisely place your flies into the right areas while not hooking up with the trees behind you. The trout do not run that large, but they more than make up for it with how perfect they look. Wild trout are extremely spooky by nature, so approach and fish the river as stealthily as you can. Most fishing on the Lyn is very cheap and easily arranged.

There is also some saltwater fishing at the mouth of the river in Lynmouth. Mullet, particularly, will enter the lower part of the river on a high tide, and they can also be groundbaited in along the rocky coastline east and west of the village. Be very careful if wandering along the shoreline at low tide not to get cut off by a rising tide. North Devon is also good for bass fishing from the shore, especially if you have some moderate onshore conditions putting some life and fizz on the water.

Best times to fish
Boat fishing takes place all year round, but it is very weather dependent. May until the end of September is best for the big conger eels

Fishing methods
Bait and lure

Getting there
About four hours from London, very easy

Tips and tricks
Braided lines help to reduce the amount of weight you will need to fish with

PLYMOUTH, ENGLAND
Weather and tides are everything when wreck fishing from this historic English port

For many years the historic port of Plymouth in the south-west of England has been right at the forefront of modern charter boat fishing. Within a day's fishing, you can come across numerous wrecks and reefs holding species of fish such as conger eels, cod, ling and pollock, as well as bass and even blue sharks. As electronic navigational aids began to improve in the late 1960s, so the many professional charter boats began to explore and open up far more of their local waters for sport fishing, and still now Plymouth is known as one of the must-fish ports in the UK. The south coast of the UK as a whole offers some very good wreck and reef fishing, and on balanced fishing tackle you can experience some wonderful sport fishing.

The two main factors to charter boat fishing from a port like Plymouth are wind and tides. If the wind is too strong then the boats cannot fish offshore where the wrecks and reefs are, but there is often some shelter and back-up fishing within the confines of Plymouth Sound itself. When it comes to the UK weather, there is no predicting when the winds might be at their lightest but, bearing in mind that there is all-year-round boat fishing, you might well be lucky and get out at almost any time. The best thing to do is to ring your chosen skipper, talk through available dates and options, and speak again closer to the day with regards to the weather.

The tides then essentially dictate what kind of boat fishing you can actually do. The smaller neap tides allow the skippers to successfully anchor above the wrecks, which is especially useful if fishing for the hard-fighting conger eels that are so prevalent in these rich waters. Ling are also taken at anchor, but it is for large conger eels that Plymouth has become so well known and the best times of year for them are from May through to September. The largest conger eels tend to be taken on the wrecks where the concentration of both eels and their food supply is highest, but the extensive reef systems also throw up big fish in often shallower water. On larger spring tides the boats drift fish the wrecks and reefs for pollock in particular, and sometimes for bass and cod when they are around. Pollock can be fished for throughout the year if the weather allows, but the time for the largest specimens on the wrecks is winter into spring, and then decent fish turn up on the reefs from late spring. In summer and early autumn, the boats can head some 20 miles offshore and drift fish for blue sharks that run the currents. The whole surrounding coastline also provides plenty of shore and small boat fishing, with something on offer every month of the year.

Cornwall

SOUTH-EAST CORNWALL, ENGLAND
Classical English shore fishing in a quiet corner of Cornwall

Best times to fish
There is fishing all year round, but bass tend to be most easily caught from about April into October

Fishing methods
Lure, bait and fly

Getting there
Very close to Plymouth, many roads and paths

Tips and tricks
Look for shelter if the wind is blowing hard from the south or south-west

Not as rugged or exposed as Cornwall's famous north coast, the south coast nevertheless offers a huge range of fishing from a wide variety of different locations. The south-east corner of Cornwall is a little known but stunning area that at times can fish really well for any number of saltwater species but, as with all sea fishing, it is very dependent on specific conditions to really get it firing. There are a mixture of very out of the way, hard to get to locations and also numerous easily accessible places that can all fish well at times.

Whitsand Bay is a good south-west facing surf beach that can produce some quality bass fishing when the conditions are moderately onshore from the south or south-west. In too much wind, this largely south-facing coastline tends to become blown out and can't be fished. The various rocks and clean areas of beach between the imposing Rame Head down to Portwrinkle work well for bass at different stages of tide. The huge beach itself is popular with surfers and families during the summer season especially, so it is best to avoid fishing during the main part of the day. If you fish early or late, however, the chances are that you will end up with the place to yourself. Bass fishing at night with baits such as crab or worm can be good when there is a moderate surf rolling in on a flooding tide, whereas the rockier locations respond well to lure fishing. Rame Head can even produce sea trout in early spring, and for the most part the larger fish turn up soon after there has been a good blow from the south-west. Take extra care on the rocks when fishing after bad weather.

The rough ground areas west from Portwrinkle can all be good for bass and wrasse fishing, with conger eels, bull huss and rays to be caught at night when fishing mainly with fish and squid baits. In summer you can catch mackerel from many locations. The bustling holiday town of Looe has plenty of mullet around during the summer months especially, whilst flounder can be caught within the tidal river reaches during winter. This is a great place too to take young children crab fishing, particularly if you go close to where the boats moor up.

The Cornish side of the imposing River Tamar is not an area that tends to produce an abundance of fish, but if you want to chase big conger eels and thornback rays year round, along with some cod in the winter, then it is very much worth spending time there. The quiet and stunning River Lynher is a tributary of the Tamar that is perfect for mullet fishing from around April to November.

Best times to fish
Spring to autumn for most of the shore fishing, but the largest thick-lipped mullet tend to be around during winter. Boat fishing in the summer generally

Fishing methods
Mostly lure and bait, but mullet and pollack can be taken on flies

Getting there
Helicopter or ferry from Penzance, flights from various regional airports

Tips and tricks
Look for rotting seaweed along the shoreline and you will more often than not find mullet feeding on the maggots that are washed out of it

ISLES OF SCILLY, ENGLAND
Water, water everywhere, but scarcely another angler in sight

Situated some 28 miles off Land's End on the south-western most tip of Cornwall, the rugged and stunningly beautiful Isles of Scilly are a collection of a few sparsely populated islands and numerous other uninhabited rocks that stick out of the cold Atlantic Ocean. More famous by far for their pristine white sandy beaches, lack of crowds and bird watching, the Isles of Scilly just happen to offer some of the best saltwater fishing anywhere in the UK. The inhabited islands of St Mary's, Tresco, St Martin's, Bryher and St Agnes are like a well-kept fishing secret, and besides a bit of mainly holiday-style boat fishing, you would be seriously unlucky to even see another shore angler over there.

What makes the Isles of Scilly so special from a shore fishing point of view is that they offer such easy access to deep water so close to shore. For the most part, you will find the deepest water on the outside of the islands, facing out towards the Atlantic, and sometimes you can fish off a rock that has over 100ft of deep, dark water right beneath it. Deep water and current in a place like this is always going to be about spinning for pollack from the shore, and the Isles of Scilly are about as good as it gets. These fish crash dive in the deep water. There are a few spots where it is possible to actually fish over wrecks that are within casting distance of the rocks. Wrasse abound here, and with such a depth of water, it is perfectly possible to catch species such as conger eels and bull huss in the middle of the day.

A very useful factor to take into account when planning a fishing trip to the Isles of Scilly is that with all those coastlines that face so many different directions, you will always be able to find some kind of shelter if the weather decides to play nasty. As much as the deep water perhaps holds the most appeal, bear in mind that there is also plenty of shallow water, particularly on the inside of the islands. The terrain looks perfect for bass fishing, but for some unknown reason they are very rarely caught around here. However, you will find an abundance of mullet, and with the right weather the thick-lipped grey mullet can be fished for all year round. From the boats there is some very good fishing for both blue and porbeagle sharks during the summer and early autumn months, as well as hordes of mackerel, pollack and ling for starters. Due to so much deep water close inshore, there is rarely a need to head out that far from land.

Denmark

Best times to fish
March to May is the most consistent time, with April being the best month

Fishing methods
Lure and fly

Getting there
Denmark is easily accessible from many international airports. Road access to the coastline is very good

Tips and tricks
Don't just wade out into the water straightaway. Put a few casts right into the shallows as there might be sea trout hanging around very close to shore

DENMARK COASTLINE
Many, many miles of some truly outstanding coastal sea trout fishing

As much as saltwater anglers in North America would go striped bass fishing along the north-east shoreline of the USA, for example, in Denmark they would go sea trout fishing. It's what they do, and because Denmark offers literally thousands of different locations to fish for sea trout from the shore, there are plenty of places to tuck yourself away out of the weather if needs be. Sea trout are never going to be an easy fish to catch from the shore or from a river, but every year there are fish over the 20lb mark taken from Danish waters.

The depth of winter is not an easy time to go fishing for sea trout, but if you do manage to catch one then the chances are it will be a stunning silver fish that has decided, for some reason, not to spawn that particular year. Yet this colder water can concentrate good numbers of sea trout within the fjords themselves. You need to look for sections of slightly warmer water, although this difference might only be a degree or two, hence many anglers often carry thermometers.

It's from March that more and more sea trout start to turn up within easy casting range from the shore, and the best of the fishing tends to be around March to the middle of May. April is generally considered the best overall month. From June and July the sea trout begin to move up the rivers, with the largest numbers doing so around September and October. Although this means that a good quantity of sea trout are now congregating around the river mouths, it is without doubt harder to catch them than during the spring.

There is ample coastline to fish in Denmark, but in general you are going to find the bigger sea trout in east Sealand and along the Setvns peninsula. East Jutland is more about greater numbers of generally smaller fish, but remember that this is fishing and there are no hard and fast rules at all.

Much of the sea trout fishing off the coast of Denmark is done with lures, although fly fishing does work when conditions are favourable. Most anglers will use a fairly standard spinning rod of around 8–10ft in length, along with any number of different slim metal lures that are designed to imitate sprats and herrings. The key is to match the conditions to where you are going to fish. A gentle onshore breeze will help the fishing, but too strong a wind drives too much weed around, making the fishing very tricky. Sea trout are notoriously good at throwing the hooks, so be prepared to be mentally beaten up by these fish from time to time. They are undoubtedly worth it though.

France

Lake Cassien

Best times to fish
It is perfectly possible to catch carp all year round on a lake like Cassien, but the best times as regards temperatures and carp feeding habits would tend to be April to December

Fishing methods
Bait

Getting there
Easily accessible from Nice and Cannes

Tips and tricks
Bait, bait and more bait

LAKE CASSIEN, FRANCE
One of the most famous waters in Europe for big carp

When it comes to freshwater fishing, chasing big carp is hugely popular throughout Europe and increasingly throughout the world, and it has been British anglers at the forefront of what might be termed modern carp fishing. As much as the UK does indeed have some mighty carp waters, many anglers have for years travelled to new lakes and rivers on the lookout for even larger fish. The Lac de Saint Cassien has for some time now been among the most famous lakes for carp fishing. Heading to the warmer climes of France to fish for big carp really began to take off in the mid-1980s, and with the capture of a massive 76lb fish, Lake Cassien came to prominence. For many carp anglers, this large waterway is one of the legendary places to test their skills on the wary carp, and it still holds carp weighing over 70lb, which is a big fish in anyone's book.

Cassien is situated in the south of France, close to both Nice and Cannes. The lake is around 4 miles long from north to south and covers an area of 1,500 acres. The three arms to the lake

are well known to carp anglers. The north, south and west arms all contain different features and depths of water, and although there is a very healthy population of big carp averaging perhaps close to 40lbs, make no mistake in that fish like this are difficult to catch – a pushover they are not.

Fishing for big carp takes huge amounts of time, planning and effort, and a part of the reason that France is such a popular carp fishing destination has to be down to the warmer climate and, of course, good numbers of big fish. The ability to fish for long periods in warm weather certainly makes the task of waiting for big fish to move onto your baits much easier, and Cassien, being in the south of France, is just perfect. But if you have no experience of going to new and somewhat potentially daunting waters, then make sure you look around for a number of professional operators who, for very sensible prices, can arrange a carp fishing adventure for you on a lake such as Cassien. To be able to travel with minimal gear and turn up at the right spots at the right times is totally invaluable, and such is the growing international appeal of big carp fishing that more and more anglers are doing this each year.

Best times to fish
There is fishing all year round, but the best bass fishing tends to be from about May until October

Fishing methods
Lure and bait, but saltwater fly fishing will also work

Getting there
A short ferry journey from Quiberon

Tips and tricks
Take great care when fishing the west coast, especially due to the large swells that can roll in

BELLE ÎLE, FRANCE
A perfect gem of an island only a few miles from mainland France

Located just off the coast of Brittany in north-west France, the stunning island of Belle Île offers a glimpse of the old France, where cobbled streets throng with cafes and restaurants, and the saltwater fishing is one of its well kept secrets. In general, the west coast of Belle Île is incredibly rugged and wild, whereas the gentler east coast has plenty of more sheltered bays and beaches. Around this entire island can be found some excellent shore fishing, especially for bass, and there are a few professional skippers plying these lively waters for numerous sport fishing clients who make the easy ferry journey over from Quiberon.

The entire coast of Brittany is beset with bass fishing, from savage rock locations through to quiet estuaries, and Belle Île is almost like a miniature version all rolled into one tiny land mass. The north-west coast particularly is a place very much worth fishing, but great care must be taken on these treacherous rocks that at times are pounded by violent storms. Even on calm days a large swell can roll in, but bass love this kind of terrain. Fish with large minnows, casting jigs and soft plastics and explore the numerous easily accessible rocky platforms. At night, it is also possible to catch large conger eels with baits that are fished tight to the rocky bottom.

The east coast has a number of beaches and rock locations that can throw up big bass, and if the west coast can't be fished due to unfavourable weather conditions, then look for some potentially more sheltered spots on the east side. Winter also produces a few different species of bream from the beaches to ledgered baits, as well as the fine tasting sole. Mullet abound in the two main harbours during the summer months.

The French bass fishermen are very good at vertical jigging with large soft plastics in relatively shallow water when they fish from boats, and the waters surrounding Belle Île offer them multiple chances to fish like this. Sometimes you will end up fishing very close to shore, and big pollack often turn up on the bass gear. You will find numerous locations to go and boat fish with surface and sub-surface lures for the bass. There is always some fishing around Belle Île at any time of year, but the best of the bass fishing is from about May through to October.

Belle Île is a wonderful place to visit with the family and, if you time it right, it is more than possible to fit a few hours' bass fishing in before the day really starts. Sitting outside one of the cafes with a coffee and a croissant and watching the world gently go by is a part of what makes this island so special.

Best times to fish
Bass fishing is very
dependent on the
conditions, but it can
be good nearly all year
round if you get the right
weather and sea states

Fishing methods
Lure, bait and fly

Getting there
Easy road access, and the
main airport is Oviedo

Tips and tricks
Stay well above the sea
when there is any kind of
swell running

ASTURIAS, SPAIN
Some of Spain's lesser known regions can produce some magical fishing

Asturias is a region in northern Spain, flanked by Galicia to the west and Cantabria to the east. The north of Spain could not be any more different to the south; indeed many people go to the north to escape the almost insufferable heat of southern Spain during the summer months. The climate in Asturias might best be described as typically Atlantic. There is plenty of rain throughout the year, average summer temperatures are about 22° C/72° F, with fairly mild winters. Unlike the Mediterranean in the south, the Atlantic is cold. The main city in Asturias is Oviedo and the largest port is Gijon. From much of the rugged coastline you can see the impressive Picos de Europa mountain range reaching to the sky as a backdrop. Along the coastline is some of the best bass fishing in Europe, and in the many rivers you can find some outstanding brown trout, sea trout and even salmon fishing.

The salmon fishing season is short, from May to the end of July, and you must make sure to either look around for a local guide or secure the various permits yourself. Spanish bureaucracy perhaps will cause you to lean favourably towards hiring a local fishing guide. The brown and sea trout seasons run from 16 May to the end of August.

As much as fly fishing is an almost universal method of fishing, the way that the local anglers go about their bass fishing principally involves having to overcome conditions that are sometimes bordering on dangerous. It is a wild, untamed coastline that requires a very knowledgeable and skilled approach. However, this northern coast of Spain does produce good numbers of big bass to anglers who know what they are doing, but is without doubt not a place for the inexperienced saltwater angler.

It is important to realise just how much this rugged coastline is battered by the Atlantic Ocean, although the continual movement of water combined with such an abundance of great bass fishing ground is what makes Asturias one of the hidden gems of European saltwater angling. Local anglers will use all their knowledge and skill to work out when the bass are likely to be in close to the shore and feeding, and the majority of the fishing is carried out in much the same way as it is in France, Ireland and the UK. Fast-action spinning or lure rods are combined with strong spinning reels, and then an array of modern lures are used to fish the different kinds of terrain. In general, the often lively conditions do not colour up the water too much for bass fishing due to the relatively deep water close inshore.

Best times to fish
Winter tends to be the best time for jigging, while big game trolling is generally better during summer

Fishing methods
Mainly lures and bait

Getting there
Easily accessible from a number of southern Spanish airports such as Malaga

Tips and tricks
If you get into jigging, buy the best gear you can and then learn some proper knots. Jigging is brutally tough on fishing tackle

STRAIT OF GIBRALTAR, SPAIN
Where the waters of the Mediterranean and the Atlantic meet. Fish love it

Most serious anglers who know about fishing in Europe would regard the Strait of Gibraltar as one of the top fishing spots. Any area where currents collide is always going to be worth checking out, and in the Strait you have the warm waters of the Mediterranean literally bumping into the colder waters of the Atlantic. When you put this together with an undersea topography that is all about fish-holding features and structure, you end up with one serious place to go fishing. There are literally underwater mountains and plateaus that can sometimes force the water into such contortions that the effects can be seen on the surface. For various reasons these waters do not receive a huge amount of commercial fishing pressure.

The waters seem almost custom-designed for vertical or speed jigging. As a form of fishing, jigging, or even pirking, has been practised for a long time, but it was the Japanese who got hold of it a few years back and essentially reinvented it. In came modern braided lines, short, very powerful rods and up-to-date spinning reels that could cope specifically with the pressure. Also came the use of assist hooks on increasingly specialist jigs. This all helped anglers to fish far more effectively in deep water for serious fish, and the Strait of Gibraltar is one of those places where the ability to properly fish jigs at depth has massively upped the fishing potential.

One thing you have to bear in mind when heading out to fish the Strait of Gibraltar is that the weather can change incredibly quickly. What might start as a lovely calm day can rapidly turn into a raging gale as that wind whips between the coast of Morocco and Spain. You would therefore be wise to hire only good local skippers and their boats, and trust in their knowledge. Most of the vertical jigging in the Strait is done in deep water in depths of over 160ft where the structure such as reefs and pinnacles attract all manner of fish species. Even deeper water is often fished, although there are some very strong currents running through this area that can make it tricky at times. Fish like amberjacks, various groupers, red porgy and dentex will all readily consume vertical jigs. You can also experience some good, more 'conventional' lure fishing on or near the surface for species such as bonito and bluefish, and there is the potential too to troll big game lures for species like marlin and bluefin tuna. However, without doubt it is the ability to fish the deeper waters via jigging that has brought about such an increased interest in these fascinating, turbulent waters.

Best times to fish
Winter for the huchen, and spring to early autumn for most of the trout and grayling fishing

Fishing methods
Fly fishing, but some lure fishing for the huchen

Getting there
Either fly to Ljubljana in Slovenia, or think about somewhere like Treviso in Italy and then drive there

Tips and tricks
For the best shot at a big marble trout, find a good guide and work closely with him

SLOVENIA, EUROPE
A hidden gem within the world of fly fishing

Slovenia is a small country that is extremely rich in fly fishing opportunities; indeed, with the sheer beauty and diversity on offer, some of the rivers and scenery will take your breath away. Each waterway seems to provide its own unique set of fly fishing challenges to overcome, and within what is Slovenia's most famous river, the Soca, there swims an indigenous marble trout that has been caught to over 40lbs. These potentially huge trout tend to feed on the multitude of grayling that also exist in many of the rivers. Slovenia might not be very well known within fly fishing circles, but it is without doubt one of those hidden gems that deserves a place on the world stage.

The Soca is an alpine river that winds through some incredible landscape amongst the Julian Alps. It rises from the Trenta Valley and offers the best fishing usually from around mid-August until the end of September, but if you catch it right then it can fish well earlier in the season too. This is a wild, cold river that is inhabited by those monstrous marble trout as well as wild brown trout and some big grayling. The best fishing often requires a bit of a hike to access the water, but that is part of what makes this one of the most interesting and stunning rivers in Europe. The Soca or marble trout (*Salmo Marmoratus*) is native to the Soca river and its tributaries, and whilst at one point these magnificent fish were deemed close to extinction, careful management and protection have enabled the stocks to return to a healthy level.

The Unec river is a completely natural chalkstream from which good numbers of brown trout and grayling can be caught. It is incredibly rich with insect life, including some prolific sedge hatches, particularly in the evenings. This of course makes the river just about perfect for any fly angler who is keen on fishing with dry flies and watching as trout take them gently off the surface. Some would argue that this is fly fishing for trout as it's meant to be. There are some seriously large grayling in the Unec, and the fishing can be good all the way through from May to November. The Krka river is another fantastic chalkstream that has some big brown trout and rainbows.

The huchen, or Danube salmon, are related to the mighty taimen, which are found predominantly in Mongolia. In the Sava river and its tributaries, huchen can sometimes be caught during the winter months. They are not an easy fish to find, and fishing for them is only permitted from November to March, but it is possible to catch one if the river is in good shape. These fish are able to grow to over 50lbs, but not many fly anglers can lay claim to having landed one. To be fair though, most of the huchen fishing is done with lures.

Iran
U.A.E.
Qatar
Oman
Arabian Sea

Best times to fish
Fishing is good all year round, but the best times are around the middle of September to the end of April, when the monsoon winds are not blowing

Fishing methods
Lure, bait and fly

Getting there
Salalah is a good airport to head for in Oman, and some operations will bring you in from Dubai

Tips and tricks
Learn some very, very good knots for joining heavy braided mainlines to strong leaders. GTs tear inferior tackle to pieces

OMAN, MIDDLE EAST
These tranquil Indian Ocean waters conceal a dark secret in the shape of some seriously powerful fish

Oman, or the Sultanate of Oman as it is officially called, is washed by the warm waters of the Indian Ocean, and along much of the coastline there is virtually no fishing pressure at all. Oman is an extremely friendly and easily accessible country to visit, but off its shores swim some of the most unfriendly and brutally powerful species of fish around. Oman is fast becoming known as one of the best places in the world to go and chase really large, potentially 100lb plus giant trevally, or GTs, as they are more commonly known. You might also end up tangling with tuna, various billfish species and even some big sand sharks/guitar fish off the beaches. It is in the southern part of the country where the best of the fishing tends to take place, with the Hallaniyat Islands that lie offshore being a particularly good area to go and battle with big GTs.

There are few species of fish on this planet that will hit a surface lure with such aggression, power and ferocity as a GT does. Even with all the strongest and most hi-tech gear available, a big

GT is still going to create carnage for the lucky (or is that unlucky?) angler who hooks one off the top. It takes huge skill, determination and no amount of luck to stop a big fish breaking you off on structure. Like many predators, GTs love structure, features and current for hunting their prey, and southern Oman has all this and more. An area like the Hallaniyat Islands offers all the GT water you could ever hope to find, with numerous reefs, shallows and deep drop-offs that these fish just thrive on. It is also possible to speed or vertical jig the deeper water for various grouper species as well as for another of the world's bully-boy saltwater species, the amberjack. GTs off the top and then amberjack down deep would be enough to reduce any angler to a quivering wreck, but off southern Oman you equally stand a good chance of raising a sailfish or a marlin on trolled lures. Big mahi mahi might also be lurking around any floating flotsam you come across on the surface.

If you would rather do some shore fishing for a few smaller species that are not going to try and break you as much as a GT, then you might end up connected to a bluefish, barracuda, spangled emperor, grouper or queenfish. However, if you want more of a challenge, then consider going night fishing for some big sand sharks or guitar fish, as they are sometimes known.

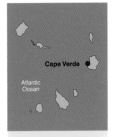

Cape Verde

Atlantic Ocean

Best times to fish
The best marlin season is from March to October

Fishing methods
Mainly lures and baits

Getting there
Easily accessible from many airports. Fly into Sal and then take a connecting flight

Tips and tricks
Marlin are of course the main draw, but find time to target the amberjack and perhaps even the big tiger sharks

CAPE VERDE, ATLANTIC OCEAN
At times the fishing for blue marlin in these waters is as good as it gets

Around 250 miles off the coast of Senegal in West Africa and 850 miles south of the Canary Islands lies the archipelago of Cape Verde, and it is to here that big game anglers come when they are chasing some of the best blue marlin fishing to be had anywhere in the world. The sheer numbers of fish hooked can be incredible; indeed back in 1997 a big game fishing boat registered the capture of 20 blue marlin in one single day, and in 2008, 15 blue marlin were landed from a local boat. The fact that these volcanic islands lie right in the middle of the mighty Atlantic Ocean means that many different pelagic species are inclined to stop off and feed in these rich waters. The average size of blue marlin is around the 200-350lb mark, and every season plenty of fish weighing 500lb or more are caught.

The most popular and well-known island in Cape Verde is Sal. Despite the fact that there can be some good fishing around here, if you are seriously into your marlin fishing then it is highly likely you will be jumping on a short flight to the island of Sao Vicente, which is where the serious big game boats ply their trade.

Although Cape Verde has some outstanding blue marlin fishing, with constant winds mainly around the force 5 mark you are going to need to be able to withstand the long, pitching days at sea required to connect with these outrageously powerful big game fish. Cape Verde is one of those rare places on earth where you might feasibly hook up to a marlin weighing over 1,000lbs.

Although fishing in Cape Verde of course centres around the blue marlin, it would be a shame not to have a go at catching some of the other species that abound in these rich waters. If you like your fishing to involve a good deal of sweat and pain then make sure you ask your skipper about doing some vertical or speed jigging for the obscenely strong amberjack which patrol the local reefs like the playground bullies that they are.

Get it right and you could also tangle with the real speedsters of the oceans, the mighty wahoo; they have been caught in excess of 80lbs in Cape Verde waters. Good numbers of yellowfin tuna turn up from time to time and can reach over 200lbs, while sailfish and spearfish can be spotted too. Boat fishing for particularly big sharks is extremely good, with the tiger shark being one of the principal quarries.

Best times to fish
September to April,
peaking November
to February

Fishing methods
Lure, bait and fly

Getting there
Not easy. Main airport
is Libreville and there
are flights direct from
Paris to here. Getting
around Gabon is not
straightforward, but it
can be done

Tips and tricks
Threadfin respond
well to soft plastic lures
fished on weighted jigs
on the bottom

IGUELA LAGOON, GABON
The beating pulse of tropical west Africa is not easy to get at, but the fishing can be off the scale

The west coast of Africa offers the adventurous angler all manner of different fishing experiences, from the cold waters of Namibia and South Africa through to the tropical conditions of a troubled country such as Sierra Leone. Many of these countries have had huge internal problems over the years, but places like Angola are now very much worth making the effort to fish. The central west African country of Gabon is a relatively stable place that has some truly world class saltwater fishing, but as with many of these areas of Africa, gaining access to this fishing is not that easy. The rewards for the effort though can be truly breathtaking.

At the time of writing there is no longer a viable eco-tourist lodge around the magnificent Iguela lagoon area on the coastline of Gabon, but it is hoped that eventually the place will re-open. However, a French-run fishing lodge closer to the river mouth is worth checking out; indeed any way of accessing these waters is better than nothing. The Iguela lagoon itself is a huge area of calm brackish water with one inlet to the sea, and is full of huge fish such as monstrous West African cubera snapper and Guinean barracuda. It is generally accepted that the cubera snappers out here are the largest snappers in the world, and there is every chance of hooking one over the 100lb mark in water that might be less than six feet deep. Guinean barracuda are also the largest barracuda species in the world, and especially in the dry season they run far into the lagoon.

Around the inlet to the sea are plenty more cubera snapper, barracuda and also a strange species called the threadfin, which can also grow very large. Generally, these turbulent waters in the mouth are fished from small boats, and just outside the inlet there are often large numbers of truly huge tarpon cruising around. The tropical coast of West Africa is frequented by the largest tarpon in the world, and countries such as Gabon, Sierra Leone and, of course, the famous Cuanza river in Angola all hold tarpon up to and over the 250lb mark. Even 300lb plus fish have been rumoured from time to time.

You can also fish the beaches directly to the north and south of the Iguela lagoon mouth, again for large cubera snapper, threadfin and sometimes the tarpon, which will come within casting range. If you are wading out deep into the murky waters, then do make sure to keep a close lookout for bull sharks, which love this kind of area. Just offshore are huge shoals of both crevalle and longfin jacks. These marauding predators can sound like a washing machine when they start killing smaller fish near the surface and will often come into the lagoon itself to feed.

Best times to fish
The drier months tend to fish best. January to March and July to October, but heavy rains can occur almost anytime. The fishing can be good, however, all year round when conditions are right

Fishing methods
Mostly bait and lure, but fly fishing can work

Getting there
Murchison Falls National Park is about a five-hour drive from Kampala

Tips and tricks
Tsetse flies are a problem at times, and it is said they are drawn to the colour blue more than any other colour, so avoid wearing anything blue

MURCHISON FALLS, UGANDA
Far out freshwater fishing right in the middle of Africa's beating heart

Imagine being the first white explorer to gaze upon the unbridled ferocity of one of the largest rivers in the world literally exploding through a narrow gap to produce what is known as Murchison Falls. You can actually feel the ground shake if you stand close to the churning water at the top of the falls, and it takes a very special fish to successfully make a living at the base of this magnificent natural spectacle. To fish for Nile perch around Murchison Falls is to experience one of the truly incredible freshwater fishing adventures on earth, where location and fish combine to take you right out of your comfort zone, leaving you with fantastic, lifelong memories.

There are two main ways to fish Murchison Falls. Either you jump on a boat further downstream and motor up to fish the pools, or otherwise you walk down the side of the gorge and fish from various accessible parts of the riverbank. The walk down to the base of the falls is not remotely dangerous, but it takes a while and, especially in the heat, it can feel like forever when walking back up again. Fishing from the bank generally does give better access to more fishing spots, particularly in the Devil's Cauldron, which lies directly beneath the falls. The water here seethes

and surges like an ocean whipped up by a tropical storm, and it takes a degree of bravery and care to actually fish here. However, there are plenty of far more easily accessible riverbank locations to fish from, but do be very careful as the water is loaded with large crocodiles. You will be experiencing some truly wild fishing in the middle of untamed Africa.

The Nile perch is a species of fish that has been caught at Murchison Falls to well over 200lbs, but as huge as that is for a sport fish in freshwater, it is not nearly as large as this species can actually grow to. More usually fished for in lakes such as Nasser, the Nile perch at Murchison grows strong and very powerful on the profusion of smaller baitfish that you can so often see shoaling up along the sides of the river. There is also every chance of hooking up with one of a number of catfish species, which can also grow very large and powerful.

If the water is not too coloured from any localised rains, then Nile perch respond well to large hard and soft lures fished at a variety of different depths. The trick is to play any hooked fish very hard in order to try and stop them reaching the fast, racing current. If a big perch gets into that current, then it might well be over very quickly. Perhaps the most reliable way of catching big Nile perch is to float fish with a local baitfish. It is somewhat ominous to watch that float start to twitch as a perch begins to take the bait and then move purposefully across the pool. Hang on for dear life if you hook a monster perch.

Kwanza river

Angola Zambia

Namibia Zimbabwe

Botswana

Atlantic Ocean   South Africa   Indian Ocean

Best times to fish
For the tarpon the best season is November to March. The southern hemisphere summer is a good time for all the other species

Fishing methods
Lure, bait and fly

Getting there
The capital Luanda is accessible from places such as Portugal and South Africa, but it is nothing if not a challenge to wade through the required paperwork

Tips and tricks
It is vital to have a valid Yellow Fever certificate if you are going to Angola and you will be checked for it on arrival at Luanda

KWANZA RIVER, ANGOLA, AFRICA
If you can get there, you will find some of the largest tarpon anywhere on earth

The Kwanza river, which lies just south of the Angolan capital, Luanda, is a legendary destination for sport fishing, but as with much of Africa it is not an easy place to get to. Angola was embroiled in a bloody and bitter civil war for nearly 30 years, but now that this conflict is well and truly over, it is perfectly possible to head to places such as the river mouth of the Kwanza (sometimes spelled Cuanza) and chase monster fish. The tropical west coast of Africa is famous the world over for being home to the largest tarpon that swim, and you can also fish for big threadfin, very sizeable jacks (crevelle and longfin), cubera snapper, barracuda and rays. Not that far offshore, especially from the capital Luanda, are almost insane numbers of big mahi mahi (dolphin fish), while large marlin and sailfish can also be found further offshore in these rich African waters.

This is Angola though, and accessing this potentially spectacular fishing ground is not nearly as easy as getting yourself to places like the Florida Keys. Africa is Africa. Most visitors to Angola will need to sort out various visas and other such required paperwork; at times it seems that

some African countries almost specialise in making it very tricky to actually go there. But it can be done, and it is a perfectly safe country to visit if you go with people who know what they are doing and can help you with the fishing. You will find a fishing lodge at the Kwanza river, for example.

The Kwanza is a big, powerful river, and most of the fishing is done either in the river mouth itself or up and down the coastline just outside. There are options to go big game fishing out of Luanda, but it's the Kwanza that offers a real possibility of catching some huge tarpon. November through to about the end of March is the best time for these powerful fish, and although several adventurous and highly competent South African fly fishermen have taken some very big tarpon on the fly in the river mouth and also way up the Kwanza itself, for the most part the fish are targeted on drifted baits and lures. There is a genuine chance of connecting with a 300lb plus tarpon around the Kwanza, but many anglers familiar with this fishing worry about how many are taken and not then released.

Numerous main species of fish can be caught within the confines of the river, especially from around July to September, but the best time for fishing the waters outside of the Kwanza is generally during the southern hemisphere summer. There is also plenty of fishing to be done from the beaches and big tarpon have been landed from the shore. Hook a monster, though, and you might just find your reel emptying alarmingly quickly.

Best times to fish
From mid-October to early April, to take account of weather patterns and the hurricane season

Fishing methods
Mainly saltwater fly fishing

Getting there
The South African company FlyCastaway will fly you from Mahe to Farquhar

Tips and tricks
Drink plenty of water all the time, even when you are not feeling thirsty. Humidity is very high, and the last thing you want to do on a remote trip like this is to end up dehydrated

FARQUHAR ATOLL, SEYCHELLES
The complete, ultra-remote Seychelles experience without the need for a mothership

Although at the time of writing all mothership operations to the most remote atolls of the Seychelles have been halted due to piracy issues in the Indian Ocean, there is one atoll where a guest house facility exists to run a land-based operation. Farquhar atoll has a landing strip for a plane and is therefore often used as a staging post for the even more remote atolls when they are 'open for business'. Make no mistake, however, that this very secluded atoll itself offers some truly world-class flats and bluewater fishing for any number of species. It is a long, long way from anywhere.

Put remote Indian Ocean flats into the equation and you will always end up with some insane fly fishing for giant trevally (GTs), which are more than keen on rampaging into the shallow water on the hunt for food. Farquhar has seen its fair share of monster GTs taken on the flats, but the fact that the fly fishing operators who run trips out here can also access the deeper water on small boats gives you another chance at taking them around the edges of the atoll before they

come into the shallows. But more than that, these boats also give the adventurous angler a legitimate shot at species like yellowfin tuna, dogtooth tuna (the only resident tuna species in the world), sailfish and perhaps even various marlin fish.

The flats fishing is what a place like Farquhar is principally about, however. Aggressive GTs aside, this enchanting atoll for some reason seems to be crawling with various cheeky but charming triggerfish. You can often see their tails almost flapping in the warm breeze as they feed head down on crabs and shrimps, yet do not mistake their hunger for them being a pushover to catch. It takes real skill to connect with these fish, and whatever you do hang on and fight them very hard as they will do their very best to run for rocky cover.

Large numbers of big, hungry bonefish almost goes without saying on a remote Seychelles flats system, but Farquhar will also give you a good chance of connecting with the almost magical milkfish. If you get lucky and find these fish in feeding mode, then work closely with your guide and you might just end up hooked into one of the world's most elusive and sought-after flats species. Keep your eyes peeled as well for the potentially huge bumphead parrotfish that patrol these warm, clear waters. As much as you can sometimes literally feel them feeding on coral as you wade through the water, they can and do take flies. There are not many fly fishermen on this earth who can say they have sight fished to and then landed a 'bumpie', as they are often known.

Angola Zambia
Zimbabwe
Namibia
Botswana
Skeleton Coast
South Africa Indian Ocean
Atlantic Ocean

Best times to fish

Shark fishing is best from late October through to early April. 'Edibles' can be around all the time, but outside the main shark season is usually most consistent. Very dependent on conditions

Fishing methods

Bait fishing

Getting there

International flights land at the capital Windhoek, and then you can either drive across the desert to the coast or otherwise catch another short flight. The main towns on the coast for anglers are Henties Bay, Walvis Bay and Swakopmund

Tips and tricks

Although the temperature during the prime fishing season often feels very comfortable, do not let this fool you. Cover up as much as possible and use very good sunscreen to protect you from potentially very damaging conditions

SKELETON COAST, NAMIBIA

Hold on for dear life as a big shark tries to pull you down the beach and into those cold Atlantic waters

Fishing for big sharks is impressive enough, but bear in mind that most shark fishing takes place from a boat that can then follow the fish if it takes lots of line from your reel. Shark fishing could never remotely be called easy, but using an engine to help gain line back is a definite advantage. Now imagine hooking a big shark off a beach on the west coast of Africa. The oldest desert in the world lies behind you, yet in front of you the icy cold waters of the Atlantic Ocean pound the deserted beaches with a relentless regularity. It is far removed from the African bush, yet still a decidedly 'could only be in Africa' kind of experience. Standing there, holding manfully onto a long shore fishing rod, something suddenly hits your bait and tries its best to drag you down the beach as you cling to the rod and do your best to set the hook. Within a few minutes you are staring open-mouthed at your rapidly emptying reel, as perhaps as much as 300 yards of line has disappeared with a big shark attached to the end of it. No getting that line back with a

boat though. When it comes to saltwater fishing, there is little to compare to catching big sharks off the beach.

Namibia is a very special place to go beach fishing, for there are not many other places in the world that offer such consistent opportunities to catch sharks from the shore. Nutrient-rich currents wash these desolate beaches, bringing large numbers of sharks very close inshore, along with huge numbers of kabeljou (kob) and steenbras in season. If there is one place where a good local fishing guide is vital, then Namibia is it. All shore fishing is based around the use of a 4x4 vehicle, with your guide often driving for miles along the beach on the lookout for the correct underwater features to then stop and target the different species of fish. They essentially 'read' the water. Although these waters are often crawling with fish, it is also very easy to get it completely wrong and catch virtually nothing if you don't know how to 'read' the water and find out where along this vast expanse of nothingness the fish will be close inshore.

As mad and fun as the shark fishing can be, at times the run of 'edibles', as the kob and steenbras are known, can be quite incredible. Get it right and huge shoals of these fish come within easy casting range from the shore, and there are also smaller shark species like the gully and hound sharks that will test any angler. This is some truly far-out beach fishing.

Best times to fish
The absolute best times
for chasing tigerfish are
June and July

Fishing methods
Fly, lure and bait

Getting there
Various ways. Some
international flights
come into Livingstone
in Zambia, or otherwise
get a connection to
Kasane in Botswana via
an international airport
such as Johannesburg in
South Africa

Tips and tricks
Stay in the boats, listen
to your guides at all
times and make doubly
sure those hooks are very
well sharpened

CAPRIVI STRIP, ZAMBIA
The receding flood plains provide these savage tigerfish with all the food they could ever need

The Caprivi Strip is a narrow wetland area of land that sits on the border of north-east Namibia, southern Angola, Zambia and northern Botswana. Of principal interest to visiting anglers is the fact that notably the Chobe and Zambezi rivers flow through this finger of land, and it would be fair to say that this area of Africa offers some of the most consistent fishing for tigerfish on the whole continent.

The upper section of the mighty Zambezi is around 500 miles long, and about 43 miles below its confluence with the Chobe, the Zambezi flows over the world famous Victoria Falls. The main fishing for tigerfish takes place around this Upper Zambezi, roughly from Impalila Island (a point of land where Zambia, Botswana and Namibia meet) up to Katima Mulilo.

The main reason that the waterways around here are so stacked full of fish is because a part of the Caprivi Strip is in essence a large floodplain that is rejuvenated each year when the Zambezi floods. As the water floods out across the plains, so the fish and crustaceans can move out across the flooded terrain to feed and breed. Tigerfish, especially, can move through the deeper channels and literally wait to pick off smaller baitfish that congregate close to the edges as the nutrient-rich floodwaters trickle off the plains. The best times for this to happen are around June and July as the floodwaters are receding.

All fishing is done from boats in order to keep away from the numerous hippos, crocodiles and elephants, although being surrounded by such wildlife is very much what makes this kind of fishing adventure so exciting. To drift down an African river with a vast blue sky overhead while a herd of elephants moves slowly along the riverbank is the kind of experience that transcends simply fishing. Watching as a large crocodile somewhat ominously drops beneath the murky surface always causes the heart to miss a few beats, but then this is fishing in Africa after all.

Tigerfish respond well to many different fishing tactics, from fly to lure and of course livebaits. They have incredibly hard bony mouths that are not easy to set a hook into, plus they jump repeatedly when hooked up and are experts at throwing the hook back at you with something approaching disdain. To see a 10lb plus tigerfish successfully landed and then returned is one of freshwater fishing's most special sights.

The Caprivi Strip also happens to be one of the best places there is to see some incredibly diverse birdlife; indeed there are over 400 different species to be found around here, including raptors, hornbills, bee-eaters, fish eagles and the African finfoot. A fishing trip to a place like this is so much more than the act of just going fishing. It is far better to just give in and let Africa seep into your soul.

Best times to fish
The season starts in mid-August and runs for 16 weeks

Fishing methods
Fly fishing

Getting there
Accessed via charter flights out of Dar es Salaam

Tips and tricks
Take a spare fly rod in case of breakages

MYNERA AND RUHUDJI RIVERS, TANZANIA
Wild rivers stuffed full of insane fish that only Africa could produce

Ever since tigerfish really became a serious and popular species to chase on fly fishing tackle, the hunt has been on for the chance to catch big 20lb plus tigers. A 10lb weight has always been a magical size to try and exceed, and it is important to note that pound for pound, tigerfish are about as brutal as it gets. The more 'traditional' tigerfish areas such as the Zambezi hold some large fish, but it was not until some adventurous South Africans began exploring various remote rivers in Tanzania that anglers began to legitimately catch those supreme 20lb tigers. These are one of the ultimate freshwater predators and they hit flies, lures and baits with a staggering level of ferocity that will take any first-timer by complete surprise. Tigerfish are so far removed from say trout that it is almost like another sport altogether.

There have been rumours of remote rivers in Tanzania holding big tigerfish for a while but, as is always the case with these stories, it is not until some adventurous and forward-thinking anglers actually go and do recce trips that anything can ever be proved. No more than a couple of hours' flight away from the bustling Dar es Salaam lie two remote and wild rivers called the Mynera and the Ruhudji. Both hold big 20lb plus tigerfish, but the fishing season for them is a relatively short one to avoid the seasonal rains that flood the rivers and render them unfishable.

This is a chance to fish the true wilds of Africa. All fishing is done from boats because of the large populations of crocodiles and hippos, but if you listen to your guide there will be no problems. It is perfectly possible to see elephants as you drift down the rivers, and at night you might hear lions roaring near to the camp. You will be sleeping close to the river where the sounds of the bush are both loud yet soothing as night draws in, and first light is when the excitement levels always rise in Africa at the start of a new day.

Fly fishing for tigerfish is all about presenting your fly as often as possible in the right areas, and your guides will talk you through where to cast and strip the fly nice and quickly. Tigerfish, for all their aggression, like to hang close to the riverbank on these remote Tanzanian rivers, and at times you will hook up on sunken branches and overhanging trees, but this is where the biggest fish prefer to lie. The hit from a big tigerfish is unlike anything else in freshwater fly fishing in that, not only does it feel like stripping into a brick wall, but also that the solid brick wall will then try and rip both running line and fly rod from your grasp. The sheer shock at such savagery can take the breath away.

Angola | Zambia
Zimbabwe
Namibia | Botswana
Drakensberg mountains
South Africa
Atlantic Ocean | Indian Ocean

Best times to fish
The trout season starts in September and runs to the end of May, but many of the dams have no close season. Best times for trout are September and October, and then April and May

Fishing methods
Mostly fly fishing, but bass can be targeted on lures, flies or baits, and the carp on baits or flies

Getting there
Best accessed out of Durban. The mountains are in the KwaZulu-Natal region of South Africa

Tips and tricks
Good sunscreen is absolutely vital, and prepare for all kinds of weather, especially the higher you go

DRAKENSBERG MOUNTAINS, SOUTH AFRICA
One of southern Africa's well-kept fly fishing secrets

Without doubt, bigger trout can be found in countries like New Zealand, but few places on earth really tingle the spine as much as Africa. This vast continent offers so much fishing, although parts of it are extremely difficult to get to. However, South Africa provides plenty of safely accessible fly fishing for trout, and the majestic Drakensberg mountains are in a world of their own.

Fly fishing for trout in places such as the American Midwest is of course a highly developed pastime, with almost an entire industry supporting it. Nevertheless, in South Africa, and even Africa in general, fly fishing is really going through a strong period of growth. These days species such as tigerfish and yellowfish are now perfectly accepted fly fishing quarries, and the trout often get overlooked.

Fly fishing in the Drakensberg mountains has so far been a well-kept secret, but it is now starting to be leaked out to the wider world. As well as a number of pristine rivers that can hold some big brown trout, there are also plenty of 'dams' in South Africa. A 'dam' is merely a lake, but several are stocked with brown and rainbow trout. It's the clear rivers, though, that make this part of South Africa so worthy of serious attention. The villages of Underberg and Himeville in the southern Drakensberg are where much of the fishing is centred around, for there are plenty of crystal clear rivers here that can hold some big wild trout. How can any fly angler not want to fish on rivers with names such as Mzimkhulu, Pholela, Ndwana and Ngwangwane? You can fish as wildly or as conservatively as you like, although the true nature of trout fishing in the Drakensberg tends to come about via getting off the beaten track. But then in an area like the Drakensberg, perhaps the term 'beaten track' does not mean the same as it does elsewhere. It is usually incredibly easy in Africa to avoid other tourists, especially if you look around for top local fishing guides who know where to find the quietest spots. Some of the dams also hold huge carp and largemouth bass, and these fish can be taken on fly fishing gear at times too.

Best times to fish
September and October
for the largemouth
yellowfish; September to
December and then late
February to April for the
smallmouths

Fishing methods
Fly fishing, but plenty of
South Africans also fish
with bait and lures

Getting there
Easily accessible from
Johannesburg

Tips and tricks
Take great care when
wet-wading not to keep
falling over the mass of
rocks and boulders

VAAL RIVER, SOUTH AFRICA
One of South Africa's best kept sport fishing secrets

There is a secret to South African fly fishing that much of the outside world knows nothing about, and the best of the fishing is easily accessible from the city of Johannesburg. Within a mere two hour drive from the city centre lies some truly fantastic river fly fishing for a species of fish called the yellowfish. They are almost like a cross between the mahseer from India and English barbel and wild carp. These hard-fighting fish are as important to South African fly fishermen as their trout; indeed fly fishing for them is increasing in popularity year on year.

The Vaal river is one of the two river systems in South Africa that holds largemouth and smallmouth yellowfish, with the other being the Orange river. The largemouth yellowfish are the larger yet much more difficult species to catch on the fly, but the more abundant smallmouth can still grow over 10lbs and they fight like hell on balanced fly fishing gear. The most common way to fish for them is upstream nymphing, but they will often take dry flies, and at times the river can almost boil with feeding fish when there is a hatch on.

The reason that the Vaal river is such a perfect habitat for these feisty fish is the fact that the riverbed seems to be made up of nothing but a mass of rocks and boulders, which happen to be the perfect terrain for these fish to root around for their food. Much of the fishing is wet-wading in the often warm waters, and great care must be taken when picking a path through this ankle-breaking terrain. There is a saying in South Africa that when God had finished building the world he dumped all the spare rocks in the Vaal river.

The area alongside the Vaal, around the town of Parys, is not far at all from the bustling Johannesburg, and it is invariably one of the best areas to fish for yellowfish. There are two distinct times of year when fishing for them is most successful and these tie in with the actual flow rate of the river. Mid-September to mid-December and then from February to late April are the most consistent periods for fly fishing.

The larger and more elusive largemouth yellowfish have reached over 20lbs on the fly, but for the most part they take a lot of catching. September and October are the best times to chase these larger yellows, as they are often known. In general, you are not really sight fishing for the smallmouths, but chasing the largemouths can at times give the opportunity to spot them and then cast to them. There are some large carp and catfish in the Vaal river system which also take flies.

Best times to fish
October to April,
during the southern
hemisphere summer

Fishing methods
Fly fishing

Getting there
Usually overland via
South Africa, although
it is possible to fly into
the capital Maseru and
hire a 4x4

Tips and tricks
Travel as light as possible
to be prepared for
accessing the more
remote areas, but also
be equipped for some
surprisingly cold weather
if a front moves through

LESOTHO, AFRICA
A pure fly fishing experience in Africa's southern heart, but it's not Africa as you might imagine it to be

Often known as the 'Kingdom in the Sky', the small country of Lesotho is located within South Africa itself. It is a largely mountainous place where even the lowlands are above 3,000 feet, and all those mountains and valleys produce a number of clear rivers that abound with trout and yellowfish. Lesotho is not a well-known fishing destination outside of southern Africa, but for the adventurous anglers who come in mainly via 4x4 vehicles, it is turning out to be a piece of fishing heaven nestled within the vast and varying landscape of South Africa.

As has happened around much of the world, trout were introduced into Lesotho rivers and have thrived in the clear, predominantly cold waters. Many areas are extremely remote and well protected, but there are also plenty more easily accessible fishing locations that can offer some excellent fly fishing opportunities. With snow-capped mountains and plenty of lush, green valleys, Lesotho is a very different kind of African experience to how this vast continent is generally perceived by tourists, and fly fishing in Lesotho is all about getting off the beaten track. The

rainbow and brown trout are found mainly in the clear mountain rivers and streams, whereas the yellowfish and barbel tend to frequent the slower moving lowland rivers.

A number of professionally-guided fly fishing operations come in from South Africa, but if you are going to do this yourself then you must look to gaining the correct permissions from the local tribal chiefs before jumping into a river and going fishing. This is Africa, and in Africa they tend to do things a little differently, but gaining permission should never be a problem. The local people are famously friendly and welcoming; indeed you should look at spending some non-fishing time in and around some of the villages. Lesotho has a mountain culture where most of the population live in small villages at altitude and then farm various crops and animals.

The Senqunyane river is a very good place to fly fish for the numerous yellowfish, but make sure to keep down low as they are likely to be feeding very close to the bank as they root out a meal amongst the boulders. Rainbow trout are the most prevalent of the trout species in Lesotho, but in a few streams like the Maletsunyane you can fish for wild browns. A good way to get around the more inaccessible places is via the local Basotho ponies, which many of the locals ride from day to day. Indeed, just going for a horse ride in this enchanting kingdom is more than worth it, although if you don't ride back at home you might not think so when you try and sit down that evening.

Best times to fish
Depending on what you want to catch, there can be some good fishing all year round, but the GTs (or kingfish) are mainly there during the winter months (or summer in the southern hemisphere)

Fishing methods
Bait, lure and fly

Getting there
Easy to get to South Africa, but then 4x4s are needed to properly access the fishing around Kosi Bay

Tips and tricks
You can sometimes catch really big bonefish on bait tight to the shore, and some locals will then use them as livebaits for huge GTs

KOSI BAY, SOUTH AFRICA
The warm, fish-rich waters of the Indian Ocean pound the beaches of this remote corner of South Africa

Tucked right up against the border with Mozambique, this south-eastern corner of South Africa is washed by a wild expanse of the warm Indian Ocean. Sport fishing here is close to legendary amongst South African anglers who know all about the Kosi Bay area being one of the top places to chase big giant trevally from both shore and boat. The giant trevally is referred to around the world as the GT, but in South Africa the GT is known as the kingfish or even the ignobilis (from its Latin name). The entire trevally family of fish is called kingfish in South Africa, for example; the bluefin kingfish is in fact the bluefin trevally.

The Kosi Bay area has a system of saltwater lagoons or lakes that run in behind the sand dunes, and these waterways also hold plenty of fish such as red snapper and grunter in season.

As much as the Indian Ocean is often thought of as a picture-postcard flat calm sea where palm trees sway gently in the warm breeze, the Indian Ocean that smashes into the shoreline of South Africa is anything but. This is a warm but brutally relentless ocean that more often than not is a mass of white water and surf hitting the many beaches, and these conditions are home to any number of oversized fish, including the GTs, some huge sharks (ragged tooth, bull sharks etc), sand sharks/guitar fish, rays, rock cod and so forth. South African rock and surf anglers specialise in fishing these kinds of conditions for large fish.

The giant trevally can be caught all over the place, from inside the sheltered lagoons to well known locations such as Kosi Mouth, Bhanga Nek, Black Rock, Island Rock, Mabibi and 9 Mile Point. They are a brutally tough fish, and if you are anywhere near rocks then it is vital to step up your fishing tackle and really pile the pressure on them. Approach feeding GTs quietly in the lagoons as they will spook easily. At times they can be found in all of the lagoons, as can some herds of hippos, hence most of the fishing is done from boats.

Bhanga Nek is at the southern end of the Kosi Bay lake system and is perhaps the most accessible stretch of this coastline for fishing. Note the word accessible though, because a 4x4 vehicle is vital for fishing around here. However, this remoteness does mean that the place is not overfished and you will need to bring all supplies with you. There are plenty of rocks and deep channels to fish baits into. Black Rock can also be good for fly fishing as well as rock and surf tactics because it offers a degree of shelter from strong south-westerly winds. For any fishing here, however, make sure you buy a permit.

Best times to fish
September to June for
the tuna, with the best
times usually at the start
and end of the season

Fishing methods
Bait, lure and fly

Getting there
Cape Town is easily
accessed from all
over the world

Tips and tricks
Think hard about setting
out on one of the tuna
trips, especially if you are
prone to seasickness

CAPE TOWN, SOUTH AFRICA
The meeting place for two different, fish-rich ocean currents at the bottom of Africa

Besides being one of the great cities of the world to go and visit, Cape Town in South Africa is surrounded by rich and varied waters that provide all manner of fresh and saltwater fishing experiences, from trout up in the hills to the powerful yellowfin tuna many miles offshore, which can break even the most experienced big fish angler. Every trip to South Africa is worth it, but Cape Town really is unlike anywhere else, and the setting below Table Mountain is quite simply stunning.

In the waters off Cape Point, the most southerly point of land on the Cape Peninsula, the cold Benguela current from the Atlantic meets the much warmer Agulhas current from the Indian Ocean. Put these two together and you are left with many factors, including the presence of huge numbers of baitfish, and for a migratory species such as the yellowfin and longfin tuna this is like raiding a free supermarket. Heading out fishing for these insanely hard fighting fish usually involves long days at sea to cover the distances required to find the shoals, but for the anglers who can brave these often tempestuous waters the rewards may be huge. The journey back to port is a good time to nurse an aching body that has been battered and bruised by a big, 100lb plus yellowfin tuna. You might well see various whale species out there as well.

Yellowfin tuna are usually fished for with conventional boat fishing tackle, but an increasing number of fly anglers charter local sport fishing boats to have a go at the tuna on fly tackle. This is some very serious fishing, and fights with yellowfin tuna can last many hours. There is not much point using anything less than a good quality 14 weight outfit, and you must expect to occasionally get smashed to pieces by fish that are sometimes just too big to land on this kind of gear. But it can be done. Sometimes the boats will fish much closer inshore around Cape Point to chase the hard scrapping cape yellowtail. It seems that most fish in African waters specialise in trying to pull arms from sockets.

The southern hemisphere winter is a much quieter time for sport fishing in the waters around Cape Town, but what they do have is a massive influx of a species known locally as the snoek (pronounced the same as the snook that is caught in the US, Mexico etc, but it is a completely different type of fish). From around May to September, huge shoals of these fish move close inshore and are generally found around 15-20m down. They are a very good eating fish and can be caught on bait, lures and flies.

Angola
Zambia
Zimbabwe
Moz.
Namibia
Botswana
Sodwana Bay
Atlantic Ocean
South Africa
Indian Ocean

Best times to fish

The main billfish (ie, marlin, sailfish and swordfish) season is from November to the middle of May. February is when virtually all the fishing peaks

Fishing methods

Lures, bait and some saltwater fly fishing

Getting there

It is a remote area, about 370 miles from Johannesburg. There are international airports at Durban and Johannesburg

Tips and tricks

Hold on tight and trust that your skipper has launched through that surf many, many times before. Exhilarating to say the least, and that's before you even put a lure or a bait into the rich waters

SODWANA BAY, SOUTH AFRICA

South Africa's best spot for big game fishing, but it's the beach launch that will have you holding on for dear life

Sodwana Bay is famous for both its fishing and its world class diving. Situated on the wild south-east coast of Africa where the Indian Ocean relentlessly washes these remote shores, Sodwana Bay is roughly 250 miles north of Durban and only about 40 miles below the border with Mozambique. Durban itself is a fantastic fishing destination, but further up the coast tends to be a prime spot for the biggest marlin. Lying in the Greater St Lucia Wetland Park, the waters offshore from Sodwana Bay are arguably the best areas in South Africa to fish for species such as blue marlin, sailfish, broadbill swordfish, yellowfin tuna and mahi-mahi. Rock and surf fishing also take place all around Sodwana Bay, as well as inshore fishing on the reefs for fish like the problematically aggressive giant trevally (GT). However, it's the way that the fishing boats get out onto the water that might well scare the life out of visiting anglers the first time they experience it.

Sodwana Bay itself is a shallow bay with a big rock spit that reaches out into the Indian Ocean, and this topography helps to provide a degree of shelter from the predominantly southerly winds that blow along this coastline. It is worth noting that along most parts of this wild coastline there are no marinas to be found. South African boat anglers tend to specialise in launching their boats directly off the beaches and, as such, nearly every boat you will see is what they refer to locally as a 'ski-boat', or in other words, a fairly short and wide (or beamy) catamaran. The skipper literally drives his boat on its trailer into the shallows and floats the boat off. Then getting out to sea is a case of him skilfully and carefully finding the breaks in the waves and powering out through them. Coming back in requires the skipper to do the same thing in reverse, only this time the boat is left high and dry on the beach by quite simply gunning the engine when you are inside the breakers and crunching onto the sand at high speed. Holding on for dear life is worth remembering if you fish out here. It is not at all uncommon for a few boats to capsize during rough weather beach launches, but they breed them tough in South Africa. Private boat owners here must pass a captain's course before they are let loose on the water.

It is rare to have to fish out of sight of land off Sodwana Bay. Deep water lies close to shore, and with numerous reefs and features to hold passing baitfish, the bigger predators are of course drawn to these rich pickings. As with all marlin fishing, patience is the key, but the average size of marlin out here is large.

Best times to fish
There is always something to fish for year round inshore and from the rocks and beaches, but the main season for marlin is September to early March

Fishing methods
Lure, bait and fly

Getting there
Fly into Vilanculos from Johannesburg or Durban in South Africa, and then connect to the archipelago via boat or small plane

Tips and tricks
If you go rock and surf fishing out there, make sure you take some decent footwear to wear on the horribly sharp rocks

BAZARUTO ARCHIPELAGO, MOZAMBIQUE

A tropical island paradise that also happens to be crawling with so many different kinds of fish

The Bazaruto archipelago lies off the coast of southern Mozambique, some 250 miles north of Maputo. Declared a national park as far back as 1971, this tropical island paradise survived all the troubles in Mozambique and remains a much sought after destination for both sun-loving tourists and anglers alike. The four main islands that make up the archipelago are Bazaruto, Benguerra, Santa Carolina and Magaruque.

The warm waters of the Indian Ocean that lap these mainly sandy islands hold any number of different saltwater species, including huge marlin, giant trevally (GT, or kingfish, as they are called in Africa), various tuna species, king mackerel, sailfish, sharks and numerous reef-dwelling fish. The bulk of the sport fishing takes place from various lodges on Benguerra and Bazaruto islands, with Bazaruto being the best island for rock and surf fishing. Much of the fishing out here is done from boats that can fish close inshore and yet still offer the chance of catching marlin and sailfish in season.

It is possible to hook the largest species of marlin in the waters off these islands. The black marlin season runs from around early October to about the end of January, and the average size is around a massive 700lbs, with fish over the 1,000lb mark being taken over the years. Hook one of these mighty fish and you could well be attached to it for a very long time.

Blue and striped marlin show up from about September to January, and as with the black marlin, they tend to come fairly close inshore to feed on the shoals of tuna. The sailfish season runs from the start of June to the end of September, so aside from February there is always some kind of offshore big game fishing to do around the archipelago.

However, there is also some very good inshore fishing from the boats, as well as the rock and surf fishing on Bazaruto. As in South Africa and Namibia, 4x4 vehicles are needed to access the best fishing, and Bazaruto Lodge provides these for its guests. Many anglers come to the archipelago for the saltwater fly fishing; indeed, putting flies down very deep on the inshore reefs was pretty much pioneered by a South African guide working out of Benguerra. On lures and flies you can catch big GTs, king mackerel (called 'couta' locally), green jobfish, any number of different trevallies, queen mackerel, as well as some really big bonefish from the rocks. Fishing big surface lures on rock and surf tackle is the way to combat the giant trevallies, which can often be found right off the rocks and beaches, but in some areas they are incredibly difficult to land. Blackfin sharks and different ray species respond well to big baits fished from the shore.

Best times to fish
Mid-October to
early April

Fishing methods
Saltwater fly fishing,
but you can also fish
lures in the deep water
surrounding the atoll

Getting there
At the moment access is
not allowed, but when
it's open your fishing
operator flies you down
on a charter from Mahe.
You then live on a ship
for the trip

Tips and tricks
Very hot and humid.
Drink far more water
than you think you
need and wear plenty
of sunscreen

COSMOLEDO ATOLL, SEYCHELLES
The gentle art of fly fishing dragged kicking and screaming into a whole different dimension

At the time of writing, this remote coral atoll that lies over 600 miles away from Mahe, the capital of the Seychelles, is out of bounds to any live-aboard operations due to the threat of piracy. However, as and when it does re-open, Cosmoledo will once again prove to be perhaps the finest saltwater fly fishing destination on earth. A part of the Aldabra chain of islands and atolls, the large Cosmoledo atoll is in fact a rough circle of nine main small islands that surround a huge inner lagoon, which at its widest is seven miles wide and more than 10 miles long.

There are no inhabitants and certainly no means of accommodation on Cosmoledo itself. Frequented by numbers of boobies, terns, frigate birds and plenty of green turtles, the only way for sport anglers to access these ultra-remote and unspoilt crystal clear waters is to join a specialist fishing charter run predominantly by a few qualified South African outfitters. However, for the moment the threat of piracy in these wonderful waters has caused the Seychellois government to suspend any permission for live-aboard or 'mothership' operations.

Within the vast lagoon lie acres and acres of pristine flats, which quite literally teem with any number of different species of fish. Cosmoledo has attracted most attention due to the outrageous number of giant trevally (GT) that can be taken on fly fishing tackle on the flats. These savage predators frequent the slightly deeper flats to hunt for prey, and they will often charge a fly down so hard that they create a bow-wave off the front of their heads. GTs on the fly on the flats without doubt provide some of the best and most nerve-jangling sport a saltwater fly angler can possibly experience. There is no other place in the world that offers such consistent sight fishing to large numbers of big GTs on shallow flats.

But as much as Cosmoledo is rightly famous for its giant trevally fishing, to ignore the plethora of other fly fishing opportunities would be a shame. When the water on the flats really shallows off and the other species feel safer from attack by the numerous sharks and GTs, it at times seems like the whole place is simply alive with bonefish, and these can get really big too. There are also plenty of triggerfish, various other trevally species such as the stunning bluefin, as well as the very hard-to-catch milkfish, which are frighteningly fast once hooked. These shy fish can be seen on regular occasions, but it is not even worth casting to them unless your guide says that they are feeding in the right way. It is all wade fishing on Cosmoledo, with your guide taking you from the anchored mothership to the flats fishing in some kind of tender boat. However, often you will have to literally run for the tender if you hook up with a milkfish to gain some line back. This atoll will open up again one day, and when it does, the fish will be even hungrier for flies than they usually are.

St Brandon's atoll
Indian Ocean
Mauritius
Indian Ocean

Best times to fish
Late September to mid-December, and then late March to early June. Timed to avoid the cyclone season

Fishing methods
Saltwater fly fishing

Getting there
A mothership operation, with pick-ups from Port Louis in Mauritius

Tips and tricks
A good pair of flats boots is vital, plus those tight cycling-type shorts to wear under regular shorts and prevent chafing

ST BRANDON'S ATOLL, MAURITIUS
World-class flats fishing for hordes of big, hungry bonefish

It tends to be the case that the further you can get away from major human influence then the better the overall fishing experience is going to be. The remote St Brandon's atoll is an extensive system of saltwater flats, reefs, channels and tiny desert islands lying some 250 miles north-west of Mauritius, and it's one of those places that requires the use of a mothership to access the fishing. You fly into the Indian Ocean island of Mauritius, get yourself down to the bustling Port Louis, and then hop aboard the ship which will take you, your fishing guides and the other clients over to St Brandon's. The mothership will be your home for the duration of the trip.

St Brandon's is so special because it has such a huge array of shallow sand and coral flats that receive virtually no recreational fishing pressure, and all manner of different species abound in these warm, clear waters. This stunning atoll is fast becoming known as one of the most reliable destinations to go and chase big bonefish in really skinny water; at times the sheer numbers of bones that pour onto the flats as the tide drops are breathtaking. With virtually no fishing pressure, these bonefish can really switch on hard to flies that are presented properly as the warm and consistent breeze whips across the shallow waters. Keep yourself well focused and you will have legitimate shots at bonefish weighing 10lb or more.

It has become apparent over the last few seasons that St Brandon's is also home to very good numbers of the ultra-spooky Indian Ocean permit. Close cousins of the larger Atlantic variety, any permit is notoriously tricky to catch on the flats, but it is more than likely that a patient fly fisherman will get multiple shots at happy, feeding fish out on St Brandon's.

This being the Indian Ocean, there are of course some very large giant trevally (GT) which, from time to time, will leave the reefs that border one side of the atoll and charge mercilessly onto the flats to hunt any hapless smaller fish that they spot. If you work closely with your guide, you will always be in with a shot at some truly colossal GTs on the fly, but whatever you do, strike hard and fight it as hard as it fights you. The need to keep a hooked GT away from any underwater structure cannot be overemphasised. St Brandon's has decent numbers of GTs around, but they are not there in the numbers to be found on the even more remote Seychelles atoll of Cosmoledo, for example. However, St Brandon's has escaped the piracy problems, and several of the fishing guides believe this atoll is home to some of the largest giant trevally to be found in the Indian Ocean.

Best times to fish
There can be good fishing all year round, but nothing beats leaving a northern hemisphere winter to head south for their summer

Fishing methods
Lure, fly and bait

Getting there
Male International is the airport, with regular flights to and from Dubai, for example

Tips and tricks
Look around for some high quality travel-type rods and then sneak them into your luggage if you are heading to the Maldives on honeymoon

MALDIVES, INDIAN OCEAN
A great honeymoon destination, but the quality of the fishing might just bring about an early divorce

Famous the world over as a magical place to go on holiday, the Maldives lie in the vast Indian Ocean and is made up of over nearly 1,200 coral islands that are formed neatly around 26 atolls. All this is spread over 35,000 square miles, but still nearly 99% of what we know as the Maldives is sea. As much as this is a paradise on earth for visitors, its warm, unspoilt waters also abound with vast numbers of fish, and if you go with the right operator and people then the fishing trips can be a wonderful mix of all kinds of fishing.

With this much water around and with such a variety of features to fish over, the Maldives really is a fishing destination that can work very effectively for all kinds of anglers. Fly anglers will find pristine flats that abound with different trevally species, the incredibly cheeky and dastardly triggerfish, some bonefish and even milkfish. It would also be a huge amount of fun to wander these deserted flats with light lure fishing gear.

If jigging is your thing, then you will think the Maldives heavenly. There are so many reefs and drop-offs to fish over, and species of fish to catch include the hard-fighting dogtooth tuna, numerous trevally species (including the daddy of them all, the GT), groupers, snappers and many other weird and wonderful reef-dwelling stunners.

The more deserted waters of the Indian Ocean are always going to be good places for popping with big surface lures for fish like GTs, dogtooth tuna, snappers, groupers and even some of the yellowfin and big eye tuna. Go fully prepared to deal with some large powerful fish and you will reap the rewards both inside the sheltered lagoons and close to the drop-offs. Trolling these warm waters can throw up serious numbers of sailfish for both conventional and fly anglers, as well as black and blue marlin, dorado (mahi mahi), wahoo and tuna.

There are not that many places out there which truly offer world-class fishing for so many different species via so many different methods. The fact that the Maldives can cater so effectively to so many kinds of anglers is a big part of what makes these waters extra special. You never quite know what might jump on the end of your line and start emptying your reel at a somewhat alarming rate of knots. Some of the most successful fishing operations around the Maldives function from a mothership, and this is often the best way, for such a variety of fishing becomes so imminently achievable. The angler who manages to combine a honeymoon with all this world-class fishing and yet still comes back a happily married man or woman deserves a big pat on the back.

Ascension Island

South Atlantic Ocean

Best times to fish
The marlin season tends to run from November to April

Fishing methods
Bait and lure principally

Getting there
On the military flight that serves the Falkland Islands

Tips and tricks
Do exactly as your skipper says when chasing the marlin, for this is a very specialist kind of fishing

ASCENSION ISLAND, SOUTH ATLANTIC OCEAN
Unquestionably some of the most consistent big game fishing around

The remote Ascension Island is a mere 34 square miles in size and it lies in the south Atlantic, almost mid-way between the west coast of Africa and northern Brazil, some 500 miles south of the equator. The island was originally uninhabited due to there being no natural source of fresh water, but for some years now it has held a military base that acts as a staging post between the UK and the Falkland Islands after US military personnel constructed a runway shortly after the end of World War II. The only UK flight to Ascension lands at Ascension and then continues on to the Falklands. The population of Ascension is made up of British and American military personnel along with a number of people principally from St Helena, an island south of Ascension, who run the various organisations and services on the island. There is no unemployment, as other than visiting as a tourist, one cannot remain on the island without a work contract.

For many years the only fishing that was ever heard about was from military personnel landing plenty of tuna very close in shore, and it was not until early 2002 that the Island Administrator successfully gained permission from the military to try and open up the local waters to visiting anglers after further, incredible reports of sharks, tuna, marlin and swordfish. For many years no tourists were allowed to go to Ascension unless they were in transit to St Helena or the Falklands.

The first serious attempts at sport fishing Ascension waters started only in November 2002, and very quickly it became evident that this remote island was one of the most important and consistent marlin fishing locations in the world. From the start, the few professional angling boats found big numbers of 600lb plus blue marlin, with the magical 1,000lb mark being achieved not long afterwards. Aside from the marlin, anglers found excellent numbers of 200lb plus yellowfin tuna, dorado, massive six-gilled sharks, wahoo and even monster amberjack on vertical jigging gear. The marlin season tends to begin around the end of November and run through to mid-April, but there is no doubt that blue marlin and tuna in particular can be caught at other times.

Most of the sport fishing takes place either from the few professional big game boats or from the numerous local boats that can successfully fish the inshore waters for the tuna especially. There is also some very good fishing from the shore as well, but it is strongly advised to exercise real caution with the oceanic swells that can roll in. Notably December is the time when most of the larger swells occur. Temperatures fluctuate between 20°C and around 30°C (68-86°F), but this warmth is often lessened by the wind. With some luck it is possible to connect with fish such as sharks, tuna and even amberjack from the shoreline, but successfully landing them is another matter entirely.

Kola peninsula

Russia

Best times to fish
The season generally runs from June to September, and the rivers will all fish differently during these months. In general they will fish better into July as the water levels stabilise

Fishing methods
Fly fishing

Getting there
Generally helicopter access out of Murmansk

Tips and tricks
Make sure you book your salmon fishing trip through recognised fly fishing operators who work closely with their Russian counterparts on the ground

KOLA PENINSULA, RUSSIA
There is Atlantic salmon fishing, and then there is Atlantic salmon fishing on the Kola peninsula

There is no doubt that the remote Kola peninsula offers the best and most consistent fly fishing for Atlantic salmon to be found anywhere on earth. A few other locations might well throw up bigger fish from time to time, but nowhere other than the Kola, as it is known, can profess to having so many outstandingly good salmon fishing rivers. The Varzuga river, for example, lays claim to being the most prolific salmon river on earth. Any angler with a serious interest in Atlantic salmon fishing has either been to the Kola, has put it on his list of must-do destinations, or is spending far too much time dreaming about going there.

It has only been since Russia began to allow access to this remote region that fly anglers could really start to find out whether the rumours of outstanding Atlantic salmon fishing were indeed true. The majority of the Kola peninsula lies above the Arctic Circle. It juts out in the White Sea and is roughly the same size as Scotland. There are few people and very few roads, and most fly

anglers come in via helicopter out of Murmansk. The Kola peninsula offers such good salmon fishing precisely because it is not easy to get to and much protection is afforded to the fish themselves.

A number of now world-famous salmon rivers are fished on the Kola, and each one offers a different kind of experience. Rivers such as the Ponoi, Varzina, Yokanga, Varzuga, Umba, Litza, Kola and Kharlovka at times seem like they are literally full to bursting with Atlantic salmon; indeed several fly anglers could reminisce on how Scotland used to have runs of fish like this.

Some of the rivers are famous for producing less but generally bigger fish, while others are known for large numbers of smaller salmon. The Yokanga, for example, on the northern part of the Kola, is home to some huge salmon, as is the Kola, the Umba and the Eastern Litza. The Kharlovka river is also one of the well-known big fish rivers. The Ponoi and the Varzuga, on the other hand, are more renowned for their very prolific runs of smaller salmon, but even then there are 25lb plus fish taken every year from these cold waters. A fly angler might perhaps look at catching larger quantities of fish from the southern rivers before moving on to some of the more difficult-to-fish northern rivers that can throw up the monster salmon from time to time. The best fishing is rarely cheap though.

KAMCHATKA PENINSULA, RUSSIA
Incredibly remote, stunning and perhaps the best wild rainbow trout fishing that exists

There are many reasons to make the long trek to the remote and unspoilt Kamchatka peninsula, but the sheer abundance of wild rainbow trout is perhaps top of the list when it comes to thinking about going fly fishing here, together with steelhead, char and various Pacific salmon species. Kamchatka has not been on the angling map for long as the whole region was essentially closed to visitors (this 160,000 square mile wilderness was once a Russian military zone). However, as the Soviet Union began to break up in 1991 and a number of the border controls started to be relaxed, the most adventurous of anglers began to venture into this land and found the kind of fishing that had been rumoured for years.

In an area this vast and this wild, choosing where to fish is not going to be easy, but it is imperative to understand that anglers do not simply walk into Kamchatka and start fishing. To access waters as remote and untouched as these, you need to fish with a select few operators who are well established and experienced at running fly fishing operations within Kamchatka. Perhaps the two most famous rivers to fly fishermen would be the Zhupanova and the Sedanka, and both of them provide the kind of fishing holiday that will live with an angler forever. They are delightfully different though in the kind of experience they can offer.

The rainbow trout that swim in the Zhupanova river tend to be sizeable fish that fight like crazy, but because they are large you are not going to catch so many of them. To watch as a big rainbow trout chases a mouse pattern fly right across a pool leaves most first time Kamchatka visitors open-mouthed. Within these cold waters there are also plenty of char, various Pacific salmon species, depending on the time you go, as well as any number of Dolly Varden.

The Sedanka river is the one where anglers go if they want to catch literally so many rainbow trout that their arms are ready to fall off by the end of the day. The rainbows will mostly be in the medium-sized bracket (averaging maybe 19 inches in length, with plenty going over 20 inches), but the sheer number of fish that can rise to dry flies makes this some of the finest rainbow fishing on earth. Skated mouse patterns will work for these fish, but there are also good insect hatches on both the rivers when conditions are favourable. The Sedanka is a 100-mile long true spring creek and is therefore going to be very fishable nearly all the time during the season. Some visitors have stated that this magical waterway might well be the finest trout stream on earth.

Russia

Delger-
Muron river

Mongolia

China

Best times to fish
Mid-June to mid-July
and then through
September on the
Delger-Muron river

Fishing methods
Mainly fly fishing, but the
taimen can also be fished
for with lures. Single
barbless hooks only on
flies and lures

Getting there
Accessed out of the
capital Ulaanbaatar –
a flight to Muron and
then a truck journey
to the river

Tips and tricks
Pack a very good
quality sleeping bag
if you're going for the
rafting and camping
option. In September,
especially, it can get
very cold at night

DELGER-MURON RIVER, MONGOLIA
Remote fly fishing for the biggest trout species in the world

There are plenty of fish that might be classed as epic to fish for and catch, but some species attain the legendary status. And the taimen is just that fish. Mistakenly believed by many to be an ancient salmon species, in fact the taimen is the largest trout species there is, and the wilds of Mongolia happen to be just about the best place on earth to chase them down. You can catch trout all over the world, but the taimen is a slow-growing behemoth of a fish that likes wild, cold rivers with a good head of prey fish for them to feed on.

The Delger-Muron river runs through a part of Outer Mongolia, and the fishing can be so good principally because it is not an easy place to get to and there is virtually nobody out there. This is wilderness fishing in the truest sense of the word. Forget all about electricity, mobile phones, internet connections and newspapers, and instead head out across the vastness of the Mongolian steppe and be taken in by the sheer quiet emptiness of it all. The sections of the Delger-Muron river that are fished for taimen the most run very cold and very clear, and due to weather, the season for fishing is fairly brief. The purest way to fish for taimen is to fly fish with either single-handed or double-handed rods, depending on the size of the stretches of river you are fishing and the water you need to cover to find the fish. Taimen are not remotely easy fish to catch, but the whole point of adventures like this is to immerse yourself in a proper wilderness and then glory in such a historic, legendary species of fish as the taimen.

You can generally choose between staying at a fixed ger camp and fishing the waters within walking distance or, better still, go for the rafting and camping option that allows you to fish miles and miles of pristine water as you move steadily downstream. Eating your supper, which has been cooked over a roaring camp fire, as a blanket of stars cloak you overhead is just about the perfect adventure. Move down with the rafts each day, fish new water, stop for lunch on the riverbank, and collapse into your tent each night in an exhausted state of bliss.

Whilst taimen are not easy fish to catch, rivers such as the Delger-Muron happen to be crawling with serious numbers of the smaller lenok; even on their own, this fly fishing could be rated as a world class trout fishing experience. If the taimen are the pinnacle, then the lenok offer the chance to really just revel in catching plenty of fish in such staggering surroundings.

Best times to fish
Mid-January to mid-March to take advantage of low water levels

Fishing methods
Mainly bait, but lure and fly can also work

Getting there
Accessed out of Bangalore, usually via trucks to the river

Tips and tricks
It can get very, very hot. Drink lots of water and wear light clothes

CAUVERY RIVER, INDIA
India's legendary freshwater giant swims in some seriously inaccessible waters

If the Cauvery is one of the mighty southern Indian rivers, then the principal fish species that swims in its waters is one of the most famous and majestic freshwater fishing quarries there is. The legendary mahseer is a fish that most keen freshwater anglers will have heard about, and it is the one single species that inspires so many people to make the journey to different parts of India and tangle with this river monster.

Mahseer grow big for starters; indeed a few fortunate fishermen have caught some weighing over 100lbs. Also, they specialise in inhabiting some of the most awkward to get to and trickiest water to fish that you can possibly imagine. Think about massive boulder fields where it seems that even crocodiles tend to avoid, with the warm water being squeezed in various torrents through any available gaps, and this is the place your local guide will most likely take you to stake your claim for a mahseer. Put together the mahseer's potential size, the area of the Cauvery they inhabit and the fact that they fight very hard once hooked and it's easy to understand the legendary reputation these fish have held for so long now. Many are the tales of having to jump in a coracle and chase a big mahseer downriver.

The mahseer of northern India tend to be much sleeker and smaller than their southern cousins, for the rivers coming out of the Himalayas are generally not as large and are also somewhat colder. A river like the Cauvery in the south is perfect for larger mahseer, but as is usual, you will do much better to get as far away from large populated areas when thinking about going fishing for them. There have always been problems with poaching of these magnificent fish, but if you go to the right areas and fish with reputable companies and their guides, then you are in with a very good chance of some quality fishing.

Usually these larger southern mahseer are fished for with bottom-fished baits (ragi paste and smaller fish), which your guide will tend to cast into the nastiest looking ground there is, but it is possible to take them on heavier lures that can swim well in turbulent water. Mahseer will take flies, but generally the more successful fly fishing for them is done in the north where you can find clearer water; the thought of actually hooking a really big mahseer in such ground on fly gear perhaps does not bear thinking about. The Cauvery river also holds some different carp and barbel-like species of fish, but any anglers in this part of India will be chasing mahseer and looking to take home their own part of the legend that surrounds this fishing.

India

Andaman Islands

Sri lanka

Indian Ocean

Best times to fish
Most operators run
a generally short
season from around
January to April

Fishing methods
Lure and bait, with some
fly fishing opportunities

Getting there
Via Chennai in India
to Port Blair in the
Andaman Islands

Tips and tricks
You must have an Indian
tourist visa to access the
Andaman Islands

ANDAMAN ISLANDS, INDIAN OCEAN
A great place for the wholesale destruction of fishing tackle

The archipelago of over 300 islands that makes up the Andaman Islands lies just over 400 miles from Phuket in the Indian Ocean. Only since 1993 has the Indian government allowed any kind of diving or sport fishing to take place here, but these magical islands are fast becoming one of the must-fish destinations for numerous species of hard-fighting saltwater fish, especially the incredibly powerful dogtooth tuna and giant trevally. There is very little commercial fishing pressure in and around the islands.

Some very good big game fishing can be enjoyed in these waters, particularly along the west and east coastlines of the Barren Islands, for example, where some spectacular drop-offs pull in species such as black and blue marlin, sailfish, wahoo, king mackerel and swordfish. In some places the water drops to nearly 6,500 feet deep. Much of the big game fishing involves trolling lures through these wild waters. The majority of fishing operations that now work in these remote areas are based around a live-aboard concept, with pick-ups taking place from Port Blair.

The Andaman Islands are really gaining a world-class reputation for the more inshore-based reef and rock fishing, where saltwater junkies can cast big surface lures for species like mangrove jacks, coral trout, groupers and, of course, the giant trevally (GTs). There are some monster GTs in these warm waters, but it is vital to either take some brutally tough gear or liaise closely with your chosen operator to make sure that they are carrying the right fishing tackle. GTs are notoriously hard on fishing gear that is not up to the job, and there are plenty of tales out there of monster fish which have smashed anglers' tackle as much as they have their dreams.

The dogtooth tuna are most often caught using vertical or speed jigging techniques, and there are also large numbers of the migratory yellowfin tuna in these waters. Dogtooth tuna can at times be enticed up to take surface lures, but jigging with very powerful gear is perhaps the best method of catching them. Other species that can be taken using these techniques include various groupers, green jobfish, GTs and alternative trevally species (bluefin etc), and even sharks that might well try and 'remove' your fish from the lure. There are also various opportunities to try some shore fishing in these near-virgin waters, especially around first and last light, but make sure to work closely with your fishing operator on where to go and what to try for. The amazing volcanic topography of this unique archipelago really does provide a home for some outstanding fishing at times.

Marquesas Islands

Best times to fish
Good fishing all year round, depending on the weather. Relatively dry, with most rain in the middle of the year

Fishing methods
Lure, bait and fly

Getting there
Fly there from Tahiti, which in itself is a long way from most places

Tips and tricks
Watch out for sharks if you are storing livebaits in a container in the sea. It is perhaps worthwhile taking items such as DVDs to trade with the locals for some boat time

MARQUESAS ISLANDS, PACIFIC OCEAN

About as far away from anywhere as you can get on this earth, and the fishing reflects this remoteness

A very long way from almost anywhere, the remote Marquesas Islands sit in the Pacific Ocean, over 900 miles north-east of Tonga. An overseas territory of France, only six out of the 12 islands are inhabited. Getting there is not remotely easy, but you will experience some truly exceptional sport fishing if you make it to these stunning islands.

An abundance of tuna swim around these islands, and to any sport angler these fish are high on the list of species to target. The fight from a tuna is unmistakable; indeed some anglers might end up trying not to hook too many of the bigger ones because of the pain involved in attempting to land them. The smaller tuna tend to be the kawakawa, and these will run in huge schools along the rocky edges of the islands as well as smashing into shoals of smaller baitfish just offshore. As with this kind of fishing all over the world, look for feeding birds and more often than not you will find the predatory fish killing or working the smaller ones from below. The various tuna species will usually come right out of the water in their eagerness to hunt prey, but you still need to approach the shoals very quietly.

Plenty of the much larger yellowfin tuna can be found in these warm waters, and do not be at all surprised if they attack any smaller kawakawa that you might have hooked. Some anglers

report problems with trying to catch the kawakawa to use for bait, not because they can't find them, but rather the aggressive yellowfin can be so prevalent that they will sometimes rip most of them off the hooks before you can land them. Shadow the kawakawa shoals and you will more than likely find the larger yellowfin.

This is the remote Pacific Ocean, which means that there are some very large giant trevally around. GTs often respond well to big poppers; indeed it's one of the most exciting ways to fish. Watching these monsters smash into topwater lures is scary at the best of times, and even more so when that lure is attached to the end of your line. Hang on tightly and do your best to keep the GTs away from any underwater structure, for they fight very hard. Trout in a chalkstream supping tiny dry flies off the top they are not. You will also find plenty of the achingly beautiful bluefin trevally in amongst the GTs.

There are endless possibilities to hook fish of a potentially alarming size from the shore, for these volcanic islands plunge into some serious depths. You never quite know what you might hook and there is every chance of connecting with a fish like the dogtooth tuna. Fish such as these patrol the waters and can be caught just as easily offshore if you can find some local fishermen to take you out. The people here are very friendly, so ask around for the chance to have a go at marlin, sailfish, swordfish and mahi mahi, as well as the wahoo and tuna species. There are any number of different fish to try and catch on light gear, either from the boat or by hiking to remote points and out of the way beaches, but be constantly aware of the huge numbers of sharks that will home in on chum and livebaits. These islands offer some wild, untamed fishing where you never quite know what might happen.

Best times to fish
October to April for
the hira-suzuki

Fishing methods
Lure fishing is huge
in Japan

Getting there
Numerous international
flights to various
Japanese airports

Tips and tricks
Long-casting floating
minnows that dive
down to no more than
about 3ft work well for
the hira-suzuki. Look for
lures from around
4-6 inches long

SOUTH-WEST COASTLINE, JAPAN
Ultra-modern lure fishing gear pressed into service right in amongst the tumbling white water

Most of the western world seems to have little idea that sport fishing in Japan is simply huge. The Japanese even have entire magazines and ranges of fishing tackle that revolve around sport fishing for squid, for example. Sea bass fishing is a particularly large branch of saltwater fishing in Japan, and around this there is an immense amount of development with regards to rods, reels, lure and techniques. From the fishing point of view, there is some outstanding fishing to be had, and the hira-suzuki (a kind of sea bass in Japan), found predominantly along the southern and south-western coastline of the country, is a hugely exciting prospect.

The hira-suzuki is a shy fish that prefers to come close inshore to feed when there is a bit of a sea running. This creates plenty of turbulence and white water in which this predator can more easily ambush its prey. The other principal species of sea bass in Japan are the maru-suzuki and the tairiku-suzuki, and it's the maru-suzuki that is in fact the most commonly targeted sea bass. But the hira-suzuki presents a real challenge when it comes to fishing such lively conditions. You need to get right in amongst it to catch this fish.

On the west coast, the best winds to fish in are about a force 4 to 5 onshore, and this means from a south round to a north-westerly direction. A swell that is driven in by these winds really helps to impart plenty of 'life' to the water and give the hira-suzuki enough confidence and cover to feed close to the shoreline. Fishing with all manner of modern sub-surface minnow-type bass lures is one of the best ways to go about tempting these sea bass out from the cover of the rocks, and in Japan there is a whole industry concentrated around lure fishing. It is easy to get hold of very specialist rods, reels, lines and lures for sea bass fishing like this, and there is even plenty of proper clothing you can wear to help protect you. Many local anglers wear wetsuit-type leggings along with a specialist lure fishing vest that often has good flotation properties to help them float if they happened to fall off the rocks.

If the thought of fishing this close to lively sea conditions worries you, then there is plenty of much safer and more easily accessible saltwater fishing for the more prevalent maru-suzuki. They can be fished for nearly all around the coastline of Japan, from rocks, beaches, estuaries and harbours, both on boats and from the shore.

Best times to fish

For the black marlin it is October to December, and for the Coral Sea popping and jigging trips there can be good fishing all year round if the weather permits

Fishing methods

Lure, bait and some fly fishing

Getting there

This very much depends on what kind of trip you end up doing, but generally Cairns is a good base – from here liaise with the operator for further fly-out options

Tips and tricks

Be very realistic about your ability and then make sure you go for the right kind of trip. Days and days of heavy duty popping and jigging can be physically very demanding

CORAL SEA, AUSTRALIA
One of saltwater fishing's final frontiers.
Far away. Far out. Epic

There is possibly no place like the Coral Sea when it comes to remote saltwater fishing. Located some 300 miles off the coast of Queensland in Australia, this warm sea is a World Heritage Site, and to fish a place like this requires a serious outfitter who knows how to provide all the necessary facilities to access these remote waters. It almost goes without saying that fishing out here is done via a mothership and then tender boats from which to go fishing. An enormous variety of fish inhabit the Coral Sea, but some very serious gear and techniques are needed to catch them.

What makes the Coral Sea so special from an angling point of view is firstly its remoteness and secondly the fact that these waters are literally crawling with submerged atolls, reefs, islands and other such structures. The fishing for pelagic species like marlin, sailfish and yellowfin tuna is incredible, but the Coral Sea is perhaps best known for the amazing quality of its giant trevally (GT) and dogtooth tuna fishing. It is without doubt one of the places to put on any dream GT fishing trip list, and the outfitters involved must be credited with the amount of exploration and work they have put into bringing a destination like this within the reach of adventurous anglers.

It is a proven fact that parts of the Coral Sea, especially the waters around Cairns and Lizard Island, further north, are the best places to chase the elusive 'grander' black marlin. Big game fishing is called just that for a reason, and over 70% of black marlin weighing 1,000lbs or more have been taken from these waters. Time on the water with a good skipper gives you the best chance of catching a black marlin, but be prepared to pay for however long it takes.

The Coral Sea is well-known amongst those anglers who harbour any kind of desire to chase after plenty of big GTs. The numbers and average sizes of GTs caught (and of course released) in the remote parts of the Coral Sea almost defy belief, and now legendary places like Bugatti Reef, Black Reef, Crab Reef and the Capricorn Islands are but some of the destinations that you might end up fishing. However, perhaps what all this GT fever does do is detract slightly from the other wonderful species of fish that can come up and take poppers or stickbaits. Fish such as red bass, coral trout, monster dogtooth tuna, purple cod, wahoo, sailfish, green jobfish, various kinds of big groupers and even maori wrasse are a more than welcome surprise when fishing these stunning waters, but of course you need to be prepared for the fact that most things with fins are going to try and pull your arms off. Vertical or speed jigging for a big dogtooth tuna, for example, is going to cause any angler a little bit of grief.

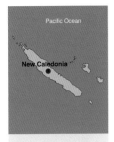

Pacific Ocean

New Caledonia

Best times to fish
May to December
tends to be best for the
bonefishing. GTs can be
caught all year round

Fishing methods
Lure, fly and bait

Getting there
The capital, Noumea,
is just over two hours
flight time from
Sydney or three hours
from Auckland

Tips and tricks
Buy the best spinning
reels you can afford if you
intend to mess with big
GTs, and then wind that
drag down tight

NEW CALEDONIA, PACIFIC OCEAN
Don't let the lovely warm temperatures lull you into thinking that the fish are going to be nice to you

Nearly 1,000 miles east of Australia lies the archipelago of New Caledonia. This part of the world really became known to anglers because of stories filtering through of pristine saltwater flats which held some huge bonefish. Over the last few years though, New Caledonia has fast emerged as one of the most consistent places in the world to go popping for enormous giant trevally. For some reason the standard size of GT in the waters around New Caledonia tends to be of a larger than average size, and more and more anglers are making the trek over there to see if all that expensive fishing tackle can actually withstand the levels of abuse that these monsters dish out.

New Caledonia is perhaps not the kind of place to venture off to on your first bonefish trip, for even though there is a distinct and very welcome lack of fishing pressure on the flats, bonefish don't seem to exist there in large numbers. Also, big bonefish tend to be wary fish, regardless of how many anglers they might or might not have seen in their lifetimes. Various other species of fish abound in the waters surrounding the flats and these can be targeted with both fly and light lure gear. Among them are the incredibly vivid bluefin trevally, queenfish, rosy jobfish and long nose emperors.

These warm tropical waters can also be fished very effectively with speed or vertical jigging tactics, but it is worth noting that to fish these methods properly takes huge reserves of strength and stamina. Tangle with a big amberjack, grouper or red bass down deep and your body will know all about it by the end of the day. UK anglers who used to somewhat sedately fish pirks for cod many years ago, for example, should know that speed or vertical jigging is something else altogether. Big tropical fish seem to delight in delivering varying degrees of pain to the angler connected to them, but then this far out kind of saltwater fishing attracts those anglers who are looking for an adventure.

New Caledonia is right in the middle of where the South Pacific Islands run into Australia's Great Barrier Reef, and these rich waters also prove most attractive to a large number of pelagic species like marlin, wahoo, Spanish mackerel, sailfish and dogtooth tuna. By doing your research and planning really thoroughly, you could do a trip to New Caledonia that takes in a wonderfully diverse array of different saltwater fishing experiences.

Pacific Ocean

Papua New
Guinea

Coral Sea

Best times to fish
Very weather dependent,
but in general the dry
season from June into
November is the best
time to go fishing in
Papua New Guinea

Fishing methods
Lure, bait and fly

Getting there
Flights out of Australia
make the most sense, but
plenty of the best fishing
is a mission to get to

Tips and tricks
If you can pull line off
your reel by hand, then
you need to tighten down
much more when chasing
the PNG black bass

PAPUA NEW GUINEA
The PNG black bass is reputed by some to be the hardest fighting freshwater fish in the world

Pound for pound the black bass of Papua New Guinea are reputedly among the most savage fighting freshwater fish that exist. Even though they do not grow much bigger than 50lbs, the PNG bass, as they are often called, are experts at literally taking anglers' gear and making a complete mockery of it. Some anglers maintain that no other freshwater fish fights as hard as the PNG bass. These magnificent brutes are not easy to locate and you will need to travel to some remote parts of Papua New Guinea to get in amongst the best of the fishing. Once you have found them though, getting these hooked fish out of their snaggy lairs is another matter altogether. You tend to play a fish like a trout, but a fish like the PNG bass brutalises you and your ego. However, if you give as good as you get, you might be in with a chance. It is not surprising that some anglers liken this unique freshwater fishing to chasing GTs or amberjacks in saltwater.

Papua New Guinea forms the eastern section of what is the second biggest island in the world (New Guinea), and it is one of the most diverse countries on earth as regards its culture; indeed there are over 800 indigenous languages in a population that is just under 7 million people. Papua New Guinea also encompasses over 600 offshore islands. Apart from the legendary black bass, there can be some outstanding fishing for big barramundi, spotted tail bass and saratoga, whilst in saltwater you could connect with various trevally species, tuna, sailfish, marlin and queenfish, for example. The fishing potential in Papua New Guinea is as varied as the culture, and the best of it is going to require some potentially serious journeys into the wilds of this fascinating country.

It is only comparatively recently that the sport fishing world has stumbled upon what Papua New Guinea has to offer, although even now there must be a world of fishing still to discover in a country where many areas are just so inaccessible and unknown. The waters that surround places such as West New Britain, New Ireland and Madang are teaming with saltwater species, and the freshwater and brackish waterways near to Kandrian and around New Britain are worth checking out for the black bass. Several adventurous Australian anglers have taken to hiring motherships and doing their own exploratory fishing trips with some staggering results. To hear of Australian anglers almost ignoring huge barramundi to get at the powerful black bass perhaps gives testament to the awe these fish inspire. If you plan a trip to Papua New Guinea carefully, then you will easily be able to experience both the fresh and saltwater fishing very close together; indeed it is in those areas where the waters mix that some of the best lighter tackle fishing is found – that is if you want to give a black bass the chance to chew up your lovely light gear and spit it back at you.

Best times to fish
Very weather dependent, with two distinct seasons – wet and dry. Most of the fishing takes place from around mid-March to the end of November

Fishing methods
Fly, lure and bait

Getting there
Various driving options, with Cairns being the major town at the base of the peninsula. Flying options include Cairns to Bamaga, on the northern tip of the cape

Tips and tricks
Keep a close eye out for saltwater crocodiles, especially if you go wandering along the beaches or creeks and lagoons on your own. Cape York is one place where the use of a professional guide or fishing operator is highly recommended

CAPE YORK, AUSTRALIA

A peninsula that is crawling with fish as well as a few menacing crocodiles. All part of the experience

Situated right on the north-eastern tip of this vast continent, Cape York is a true sport fishing wilderness. There are few places on earth that offer such a diverse opportunity to target so many different species of fish in both fresh and saltwater. The distances are huge, however, with the top of Cape York being nearly 600 miles from Cairns, the last major town. The peninsula can only really be driven during the dry season from May to December, and even then the driving might border on being somewhat 'interesting' at times. You can fly to Bamaga, which lies right at the tip of the peninsula, if the idea of getting there by vehicle does not appeal that much. A few mothership operations also fish these remote waters. Whatever option you choose to get there, it is worth putting this place on your list of 'must-fish' destinations.

The Cape York peninsula gives the adventurous anglers the chance to fish the open sea from a boat and then perhaps explore the waters that surround any number of different islands. Or you may prefer to just wander up and down deserted coastlines with a fly or lure rod in hand. There are also plenty of estuaries, lagoons and even rivers to explore, and you might end up tangling

with fish like barramundi, mangrove jacks, various trevally species, sharks, queenfish, black jew fish, Spanish mackerel, blue salmon, coral trout, cod and tuna.

Cape York is a wonderful place to go and chase barramundi, which could almost be described as Australia's national fish. 'Barra', as they are known, inhabit a number of different environments, and the massive Cape York peninsula offers the lot. A place like Weipa, on the west side of the peninsula, is often regarded as the barra capital of Queensland, but of course there are plenty of other areas to go and fish for them too.

However, surrounded by a large network of creeks and rivers, Weipa is a good place to major on for the whole Cape York experience. It can provide very good barramundi fishing, although you might also be able to fish for big trevally and queenfish. Some of the small waterways hold the biggest fish. Either side of the Weipa inlet are many miles of pristine and deserted beaches and rocky headlands where the angler can sight fish to barra, giant herring and threadfin salmon. Keep a close eye out for big giant trevally and queenfish, which could well be cruising very close to the shoreline. The fly angler will get a huge amount out of fishing like this along the beaches and rocks. There are various reef systems not far offshore that throw up red emperor and coral trout, but you must also expect to hook monsters that are just not going to be landed. The main shipping channel is a notable spot to go and chase tuna, queenfish and big GTs. At times there are numerous large hungry sharks around that can be expert at literally inhaling hooked fish from your lines.

Best times to fish
Very seasonal, but October to December is when the fishing tends to be at its absolute best

Fishing methods
Lure, fly and bait

Getting there
The Northern Territory is a huge area. Darwin is the main city

Tips and tricks
Barramundi show a marked preference for bronze or gold coloured lures

NORTHERN TERRITORY, AUSTRALIA
Barra, barra, barra. Arguably the finest barramundi waters in Australia

The vast Northern Territory in Australia is generally considered one of the top areas to go and fish for its most popular native sportfish, the barramundi, also known as barra for short. Barra are hard fighting fish that can be caught in various different ways and in a multitude of locations. The Northern Territory has endless square miles of perfect barra habitat, which includes tidal rivers and massive floodplains, and a wet season that is for the most part reliable and easy to predict. Barra fishing is very dependent on water levels and conditions, and although in certain places they can be caught all year round, it is the seasons which really dictate when you can and cannot fish for them.

Barramundi are as happy in estuaries as they are in rivers; indeed as a species they will mature in the upper reaches of freshwater waterways and then migrate downstream into the coastal reaches and estuaries to spawn. They really prefer to lurk around areas of structure, such as

mangrove roots and rock ledges, hence the reason why so many big fish are lost.

You can fish for barramundi with lures, flies and baits, and this variety of methods helps in some way to explain their almost universal appeal to anglers. They are also considered a very good eating fish if they are caught from either saltwater or the tidal sections of rivers. Perhaps the most popular way to fish for barra is with lures, but it is vital to make sure your tackle has sufficient stopping power to try and protect against a big fish doing its hardest to reach a snaggy sanctuary and dashing your dreams.

The whole barramundi fishing scene in the Northern Territory revolves around the seasons. Anglers set out to fish during the wet season from January to March, but as it ends and the water levels begin to fall, they will fish mostly from boats due to the crocodiles and remote access. During the dry season, from June to September, the freshwater lagoons and rivers open up to anglers. The barramundi tend to remain in the deeper water where the temperatures are cooler. It is the period from October to December, just before the wet season starts all over again, that the barramundi become the most active as the waters warm up. Fishing in the estuaries and freshwater lagoons can be really good during these months.

Best times to fish
From about April to October, with the calmest weather tending to be around April and May

Fishing methods
Lure, bait and fly

Getting there
Generally on a boat from Denham, although there is a landing strip on the island

Tips and tricks
Watch the swells on the west coast especially

DIRK HARTOG ISLAND, AUSTRALIA
One of western Australia's hidden fishing gems

Dirk Hartog Island is in the north of Western Australia and forms the western boundary to the Shark Bay World Heritage Area. This famous island is the site of the first recorded landing by a European on Australian soil. It was Dirk Hartog, who arrived on 25 October 1616 aboard the *Eendracht*, and as much as this wonderful place will forever be implanted within Australian history, it also happens to have some fantastic saltwater fishing. The island is 500 miles from Perth, and most anglers would access its waters via the one hour boat ride from the mainland across Shark Bay.

Dirk Hartog Island is fairly long and narrow, and the exposed west facing coastline stands like a sentinel taking the full brunt of the Indian Ocean crashing into its mainly rocky shores and steep cliffs. The east side of the island is sheltered from the prevailing westerly winds and is made up mainly of shallow bays, beaches and limestone cliffs. Islands tend to offer a degree of sheltered fishing in most wind directions if needs be. There is any number of opportunities to fish from both a boat or the extensive shoreline.

Many visiting anglers are going to head for the more sheltered eastern coastline to fish for tailor, flathead and even some giant trevally from the rocks, bays and beaches. Fishing the shallow bays for flathead with light lure and fly gear can be huge fun. Tailor usually respond best when a high tide coincides with the sun going down. The wilder west coast is gaining a reputation as one of the prime locations for potentially catching big fish like tuna and sharks from the rocks, although this is a specialist kind of fishing that requires heavy gear and plenty of time. You also need to keep a very close eye on ocean swells and rough conditions, but the chance to hook up with a true big game fish from the rocks is enough to tempt a few hardcore anglers. It is the warm water of the Leeuwin Current that helps bring these enormous fish so close to the shoreline as they chase the abundant baitfish species.

The whole Shark Bay area is known as a very important breeding and nursery area for pink snapper in particular, and with some recent conservation-based methods the snapper population is extremely healthy once again. Very good big game fishing exists further offshore, and species such as sail fish, black marlin, mahi mahi (dolphin fish), yellowfin tuna, Spanish mackerel and wahoo can all make an appearance if conditions are favourable. There is, however, still a good deal more to do when it comes to exploring these magical waters.

Indian Ocean

Australia

● Perth

Southern Ocean

Best times to fish
November to February

Fishing methods
Baits, lures and even flies at times, but vertical jigging (lure) is the best way for the biggest fish

Getting there
Perth is a major Australian city and is easily accessible

Tips and tricks
This is a time to invest in the best fishing tackle you can afford. Big samson fish can and do render plenty of gear inoperable

PERTH, AUSTRALIA
Do battle with one of the true brutes of the ocean. Give an inch and you're done

Just its name should provide some clue as to what the samson fish is about. Pound for pound it is one of the toughest brutes in the sea; indeed, the word brute is a perfect way to describe these muscled fish, which are closely related to another similarly hard fish to catch, the amberjack. Fishing for samson fish around Perth and the western coast of Australia has really taken off over the last few years, with the increased adoption of vertical or speed jigging methods.

Vertical jigging is a very effective way to fish big metal lures in some often extremely deep water, and to get to the biggest samson fish you generally need to get down deep. Using specialist, mainly slender, heavy metal jigs on strong braid lines, you can now properly fish waters off the west coast that are more than 100m deep. Samson fish like to haunt areas of structure such as wrecks, reefs, drop-offs and ledges. They can be chummed up over shallower water, but for the most part the largest fish are taken in the deep water. They have been caught to over

100lbs off western Australia, and the city of Perth is one of the best places from which to head out on a sport fishing boat.

It is the Japanese saltwater anglers who should be credited with helping to significantly advance the art of vertical jigging, and this influence really started to spread around the fishing world. Anglers from all over the place began to adopt and then adapt techniques and methods to suit their own local fishing. Getting at the biggest samson fish down deep is but one example.

Fishing is all about different experiences, but little compares to dropping down a big metal jig in over 100m of water, starting to really jig or work the lure at a sometimes incredible speed, and then getting hit so hard by a big samson fish that you might struggle to move the rod from a jigging to a fighting position. And fighting the fish is just what this is all about. Anglers do not play samson fish. Vertical or speed jigging is incredibly tough on fishing gear, and the tackle is all about taking advantage of modern materials to withstand the pressure of dealing with big fish in deep water. There is no commercial fishery off the west coast of Australia for these magnificent fish, so if anglers continue to return as many fish as possible to the sea, there seems to be no reason why jigging for these beasts should not continue to be so much painful fun for many years to come.

Best times to fish
September to April in Tasmania, but the best times for different areas depend hugely on the weather and water conditions

Fishing methods
Fly fishing

Getting there
It is best to fly to Hobart, Tasmania's capital city

Tips and tricks
Polarised sunglasses for sight-fishing, and then layered clothing to deal with some pretty extreme temperature fluctuations in the Central Highlands especially

TASMANIA, AUSTRALIA
Almost every kind of trout fishing you could hope to do rolled into one destination

Tasmania is an island that lies about 150 miles off the southern coast of Australia. Although perhaps New Zealand gets the most publicity when it comes to trout fishing (arguably the finest on earth), the island of Tasmania is unquestionably somewhere completely unique for fly fishing in that within this comparatively small state of Australia there are so many different trout fishing habitats to tempt the visiting angler. It is this sheer diversity of fly fishing options that makes Tasmania one of the must-visit places if trout are your thing, and you could find yourself fishing the streams and lowland rivers of the northern midlands, lagoons and freestone rivers through to the spectacular lakes of the Central Highland region. It is perhaps these clear and remote lakes that are the showcase of Tasmanian trout fishing.

As is the case throughout much of the world, trout were introduced to Tasmania from the UK. Back in 1839 some hardy brown trout were released into various waterways and have flourished ever since. If you could condense a number of ideal trout habitats into one area then Tasmania would be it, and there are even good numbers of rainbow trout around.

Often known as the 'Heart of Tasmania', the Central Highlands is an area where the fly angler really can fish some wild, untouched waters that are difficult to reach. Of course there are a number of more easily accessible lakes and also plenty of professional fly fishing guides who can show you the ropes, but a big part of the attraction is the sheer remoteness of this fishing. A chance to fish far from any kind of beaten track is always going to heighten the appeal for many anglers.

Another aspect that makes this Central Highland fly fishing so alluring is that much of it is based around sight-fishing to the potentially big wild brown trout. A good pair of polarised sunglasses is absolutely essential to be able to cut through the glare and form a far better understanding of how the trout are moving and feeding. They might, for example, be gently taking spent spinners off the top or even tailing for grubs in the weeds, very much like bonefish might tail on the shallow saltwater flats for little crabs and shrimps. When you see huge brown trout gently cruising the margins on the hunt for food, it takes great self-control to do everything right and tempt the fish to take your fly. Sight-fishing on the Central Highlands feels almost like an otherworldly experience, and you have to practically convince yourself that this is actually Australia, even though it is so different to the Australia that the majority of visitors would know.

Best times to fish
The best of the fly fishing tends to be during the southern hemisphere summer – November through to the end of February usually offers pretty consistent fishing

Fishing methods
Fly fishing for the trout

Getting there
Christchurch is the main international airport on the South Island

Tips and tricks
Make sure not to take any wading boots with felt soles on them as their use is banned in New Zealand

THE SOUTH ISLAND, NEW ZEALAND

The ultimate destination in the world for sight fishing to big, wild brown trout. Accept no substitute

The whole of New Zealand is an anglers' paradise, and while the North and South Islands are without doubt most famous for the quality of their fly fishing, there is of course plenty of other great sport fishing to be had in both salt and freshwater. The South Island, though, is the place that most dedicated trout fishing junkies dream of heading to, and the Nelson and Marlborough regions at the top of the island are perhaps the most popular areas.

The Southern Alps help to protect this warm, dry region from the bulk of the rains, and this wonderful climate is just about as perfect as it can get for trout fishing in the almost ridiculously clear streams and rivers that largely originate in the mountains. You can catch browns and rainbows, but it is the monster brown trout and the fact that they will often take dry flies that brings most fly anglers here. Trout up to around 15lbs are caught every year in this part of New Zealand, and to see fish in double figures in water so clear is just mind-blowing in the extreme. But make no mistake, there are no easy fish to catch, and much of the fly fishing demands a very technical and qualified approach.

New Zealand offers a great mix of fly fishing, from easily accessible public waters through to ultra-remote stretches that might well require a 4x4 vehicle or even helicopter access. Be prepared to walk into many of the best spots. There are, of course, a large number of highly qualified guides available to take fly anglers to all kinds of waters, as well as dedicated fishing lodges and various other infrastructures, although if you are competent enough, then you might also consider some DIY fishing. A trophy trout in New Zealand is a fish that weighs more than 10lbs, but of course these big fish do not get so large by being stupid.

About every five or six years there is a period when the three native species of beech trees have an especially productive flowering season at the same time, which produces a larger than normal number of seeds. The mice population alongside the rivers literally explodes on this abundance of food and they will often cross the rivers on the hunt for even more seeds. In turn, the bigger trout eat many of these mice and then get even larger than they were already. If you are lucky enough to go fly fishing in New Zealand during one of these mice-eating trout years, you might well end up hooking the biggest brown trout you have ever seen.

PICTURE CREDITS (by page number)